NEW SELECTED POEMS

Christina Rossetti was born in 1830 in London and educated at home. She was associated with the Pre-Raphaelites through her brother Dante Gabriel Rossetti. Her first collection, *Goblin Market and Other Poems* (1862), was extremely successful, followed by *The Prince's Progress and Other Poems* (1866) and *A Pageant and Other Poems* (1881). She also wrote a collection of verse for children and several essays about religion. After her death in 1894, her eldest brother, William, brought out a complete collection of her poetry.

Rachel Mann is an Anglican parish priest and writer. She was Poet-in-Residence at Manchester Cathedral between 2009 and 2017 and is the author of seven books, including *Fierce Imaginings: The Great War, Ritual, Memory and God* (DLT, 2017). She is Visiting Fellow in Creative Writing and English at Manchester Metropolitan University. Her first collection of poetry, *A Kingdom of Love*, was published by Carcanet in 2019.

CHRISTINA ROSSETTI

New Selected Poems

edited by
RACHEL MANN

CARCANET

First published in Great Britain in 2020 by
Carcanet
Alliance House, 30 Cross Street
Manchester M2 7AQ
www.carcanet.co.uk

A CIP catalogue record for this book is
available from the British Library.
ISBN 978 1 78410 906 6

Printed in Great Britain by SRP Ltd, Exeter, Devon

The publisher acknowledges financial
assistance from Arts Council England.

CONTENTS

A Pageant and Other Poems (1881)

Poems (1888, 1890)

INTRODUCTION

C.H. Sisson, editor of Carcanet's 1984 *Christina Rossetti: Selected Poems*, opens and closes his introduction with a brace of striking claims. He begins by affirming Ford Madox Ford's 1911 statement that 'Christina Rossetti seems to us the most valuable poet that the Victorian age produced.' He closes by asserting that 'in her sobriety she is the most naked of poets.' Sisson was a formidable critic and his analysis is difficult to gainsay over thirty years on from his *Selected*. Indeed, it is tempting to re-baptise Christina Rossetti 'the great naked Victorian poet'. In our rather more (social) media-obsessed times, it would surely make an eye-catching tagline.

Sisson's selection was ground-breaking. If the 1970s and '80s signalled a specifically feminist recovery of Rossetti's reputation, thanks, in part, to scholars of the stature of Cora Kaplan, Angela Leighton, Sandra M. Gilbert and Susan Gubar et al, the critical revolution was far from complete. Sisson's assertion that, by the 1980s, Rossetti's high reputation was 'hardly questionable' strikes me as a little bold. Even if Rossetti's poetics – clean, simple and often unexpectedly strange – had been reclaimed as subversively feminist, the brilliant work of critics like Isobel Armstrong arguably risked providing a new set of critical constraints for Rossetti's works. With hindsight, there is something strangely bracing about Sisson's patrician, masculine voice offering leaven to the '(re-) discoveries' of feminist theorists.

Sisson's Carcanet selection includes Rossetti's long-unavailable children's story *Maude: A Story for Girls*, a piece of juvenilia written when she was about eighteen. Published in a short-run by her brother William Michael nearly fifty years after it was written, Sisson takes *Maude* as 'undoubtedly a self-portrait, and a highly critical one'. It represents a fascinating study of an upper middle-class adolescent girl's sensibility and, as William Michael notes, even by 1897, Christina's religiously motivated self-abnegation came over as a little priggish. He says that the 'worst harm' Maude seems to have done 'is that, when she had written a good poem she felt it to be good'. Unsurprisingly, *Maude* hardly represents the peak of Rossetti's powers, but it is revealing and earns a reprint here, not least because of its religious seriousness. While biographers such as Frances Thomas and, supremely, Jan Marsh have taken recent biographical studies of Rossetti to the level of fine art, Sisson brought new focus to Rossetti's poetics through his insistence that 'with any poet the starting-point, social as well as literary, is worth finding out about'.

The facts of Rossetti's life are well-known. She was born on 5 December 1830, into a prominent Anglo-Italian family. In 1824, her poet-father Gabriele fled the kingdom of Naples for London with a price on his head, and in 1826 he married Frances, daughter of Gaetano Polidori. Polidori was formerly secretary to the poet Alfieri, and father of John, briefly famous as Byron's physician. Gabriele taught Italian and published, by subscription, a commentary on the *Inferno* during a period when Dante's works were relatively unknown. He was appointed Professor of Italian at King's College, London in 1830/1.

Christina was the youngest of four children. Maria Francesca, who became a nun, was born in 1827, while art-superstar Dante Gabriel (born at the height of Gabriele's Dante obsession) was born in 1828. William Michael, career civil servant and Christina's literary executor, came along in 1829. Of the new-born Christina, her father wrote to her aunts, 'She is considered to be the very picture of Maria, but more beautiful. She … looks with that round face of hers, like a little moon risen at the full.' Family accounts of the children's life in the Rossetti home indicate a tellingly un-English milieu. In his introduction to Christina's *Collected Poems* (1904), William Michael writes:

> The children were constantly with their parents; there was no separate nursery, and no rigid lines drawn between the big one and the little ones. Of English society there was extremely little – barely one or two families…; but of Italian society – in the sense of Italians who hunted up and haunted our father as an old acquaintance or as a celebrity – the stream was constant… there were exiles, patriots, politicians, literary men, musicians… fleshy and good-natured Neapolitans, keen Tuscans, emphatic Romans… all this – even apart from our own chiefly Italian blood – made us, no doubt, not a little different from British children in habit of thought and standard of association.

Having said all this, their mother – half-English and a former governess to an English family – undertook the entire education of the girls. Furthermore, all four children were baptised and brought up in the Church of England, and it was in the emergent world of Anglo-Catholicism that Maria and Christina found the habitus of their adult lives.

Arguably, during the late twentieth-century peak of feminist critical interest in Rossetti's poetry, the intensely religious tenor of Christina's life was seen, at best, as irrelevant to her significance and, at worst, an embarrassment to be minimised. Sisson himself, not driven by any doctrinaire consideration, is honest enough to admit that he finds much of her specifically devotional and ecclesiastical verse and writings 'largely unreadable'. His *Selected* contains rather fewer of these poems than mine. I do not aim to sport with modern readers' sensibilities. I recognise that European culture travels ever further away from the kind of biblical literacy that Christina (and even Sisson) assumed. The *Book of Common Prayer* and the *King James' Bible* no longer supply a common literary substrate between writers in English, if they ever did. In offering a wider selection of her poems shaped by her Anglo-Catholicism – by turns, lavish in its devotion and, yet, austere and reserved in what it might say of the Sacred – I hope to invite readers to make faithful, yet daring readings of both her most seemingly secular as well as her vast oeuvre of devotional writings.

However, before treating with Rossetti's faith and religion, there is a dimension that simply cannot be ignored: the impact on reading Rossetti generated by the 'Pre-Raphaelite ...' – choose your metaphor here – '... Juggernaut', '... Industry', '... Behemoth' and so on. Despite the relative brevity of its existence, the Pre-Raphaelite Brotherhood, of which her brother Dante Gabriel was the most famous member, continues to exercise a significant grip on ideas about mid-to-late nineteenth century art and culture. For good or ill, any kind of study of Christina's poetry – certainly the poetry of her most-famous phase, which includes 1862's *Goblin Market and other poems* – needs to wrestle with the curious shadow cast by Dante Gabriel, the Pre-Raphaelites and their advocates into the twenty-first century. While there has been some fascinating critical push-back recently, in which women artists like Evelyn de Morgan and critics such as Joanna Boyce have been 'recovered' from the long, sometimes unappealing shadows of Millais and Burne-Jones, 'Pre-Raphaelite' aesthetics continue to operate predominantly through a male gaze, constructing women as tragic muses.

It is always risky to load too much significance on a single poem. However, *In an Artist's Studio*, written in 1856 but only published after Christina's death, is a genuinely fascinating text. It both offers some suggestive ways to delineate Rossetti's relationship with the Pre-Raphaelite sensibility and indicates fruitful directions for reading her work post-Sisson (who didn't include the poem in his *Carcanet* selection). William Michael's note on the poem in the 1904 *Complete Poems* says that this Petrarchan sonnet refers 'apparently to our brother's studio, and to his constantly-repeated heads of the lady whom he afterwards married, Miss Siddal':

> One face looks out from all his canvasses,
>   One selfsame figure sits or walks or leans;
>   We found her hidden just behind those screens,
> That mirror gave back all her loveliness.
> A queen in opal or in ruby dress,
>   A nameless girl in freshest summer greens,
>   A saint, an angel; – every canvass means
> The same one meaning, neither more nor less.
> He feeds upon her face by day and night,
>   And she with true kind eyes looks back on him
> Fair as the moon and joyful as the light:
>   Not wan with waiting, not with sorrow dim;
> Not as she is, but was when hope shone bright;
>   Not as she is, but as she fills his dream.

Clearly, given its Petrarchan form, it displays Christina in argumentative mood. The opening octave serves to set up the argument or proposition of the poem, while the closing twin tercets or sestet serves to offer a resolution. Within this structure the volta in the ninth line presents 'a turn' in the argument. If the sonnet form is, by convention, a poem of love, *In an Artist's Studio* perhaps offers an insight into the feminist edge present in Christina's poetry: for it constitutes a cutting critique of the ways in which the female model is painted, 'framed' and controlled by the male artist. In its repeated use of 'one face', 'one selfsame figure' and 'same one meaning'

Rossetti presents a female form vampirised by her brother's male gaze.

The model – and it is worth remembering that Christina herself was the model for Dante Gabriel's first completed oil, 1849's *The Girlhood of Mary Virgin* – is reconstructed as a series of ciphers and female icons ('queen', 'saint', 'angel') or merely as 'nameless girl'. The Pre-Raphaelite obsession with constructing genericised feminine beauty denudes the female body of its particularity. At the beginning of the sonnet's sestet, the artist appears as a kind of vampire-king who 'feeds upon her face by day and night'. The model is drained of life so that the artist can gratify his fantasies. *In an Artist's Studio* suggests that the 'saint' in the picture is as fixed by the male gaze as the Blessed Virgin ever was. The artist makes a dream woman for himself. She exists to look only on the artist who made her, not at herself or at the world. She embodies – as queen, as saint, as angel – 'the same one meaning, neither more nor less'.

This might strike some readers as just too much Theory, but any serious contemporary treatment of Rossetti's poetry cannot simply plot a line around it and expect to be credible. When a relatively conservative critic Valentine Cunningham says the following, it's only fair to acknowledge the force of theorised readings of Rossetti's work:

> What's striking in recent times is how post-Theory reading has opened up Victorian poetry so convincingly, and (in the best sense) as never before. [...] [T]heorized re-readings of the canon have brought in from the cold many otherwise neglected men and women [...] Christina Rossetti and Elizabeth Barrett Browning, now in the Top Team, jostling hard against the Top Three of Tennyson, Robert Browning, and Hopkins.[1]

---

1 Valentine Cunningham, *Victorian Poetry Now: Poets, Poems, Poetics* (Oxford: Wiley-Blackwell, 2011), p. ix.

For all the definition brought by theorised readings of Rossetti's poetry, I don't think it is absurd to ignore the curious tenor of her life and what it indicates about both her finest and most modest verse. If she was part of a genuinely interesting and cultured family, it is also true that there are specific features of Rossetti's life which remain fertile territory for understanding the mood and obsessions of her poetry, not least the repeated offers of marriage, all turned down, and her experience of ill-health, notably Graves' Disease and breast cancer. Theoretical obsessions with the *Text* do not simply triumph over *Biography*, though only a fool would deny that biographical details resist the critical gaze.

One tempting and certainly suggestive line through the details of Rossetti's biography is to unite it around 'isolation' and 'self-abnegation'. This line acknowledges her early formation in a sophisticated cultural milieu,[2] but reads her as being ever more directed towards her private and isolated concerns; her inner, spiritual life, as it were. This is the Christina working alongside her sister Marie Francesca (at least until her profession of vows) in service of the poor and fallen, and devoting her increasingly ill body to devoted care for her mother, who lived until 1887. This is the Christina who – despite the fame conferred by her two best known collections *Goblin Market and Other Poems (1862)* and *The Prince's Progress and Other Poems (1866)* – negotiated her inner poetic concerns without celebrity and in relative poverty.

There is evidence for this mode of reading Rossetti. Christina had her suitors, including the painter and Pre-Raphaelite Brother, James Collinson, to whom she was introduced when she was seventeen. Collinson had converted to Roman Catholicism from Anglicanism and when he proposed she

2 Including members of the Brotherhood, Italian revolutionaries, as well as Coventry Patmore, Ruskin, Swinburne, among others.

declined his offer. He reverted to Anglicanism and she accepted him. Finally, he reconverted to Catholicism and Christina had had enough. According to William Michael, her refusal of Collinson was 'a staggering blow… from which she did not fully recover for years.' In 1866, Christina received another proposal from linguist Charles Bagot Cayley. Insofar as we know her objections to him, they were based importantly on his agnosticism. A final offer reputedly came from the painter John Brett, who is the probable subject of her forthright poem, *No, Thank You, John:* 'I never said I loved you John: / Why will you teaze me day by day.'

The themes of isolation and self-abnegation – partly generated by her religious seriousness, partly by a severe self-awareness – finds a further bolster in Christina's repeated encounters with ill-health. Her father characterised his children as two storms – Gabriel and Christina – and two calms – Maria and William Michael. The latter recalled in 1904 how her 'temperament, naturally warm and free, became a 'fountain sealed' … impulse and elan were checked, both in act and writing.' Her ever deepening faith was a factor, but also surely ill-health. At fifteen she experienced a temporary collapse of health. She became ill again in 1849, before negotiating the debilitating effects of Graves' Disease and cancer in later life. The lack of contemporary details about her early collapses has been a biographer's delight, offering space for psychosexual and psychodynamic speculation. It is difficult to disagree, at this point with Sisson's insistence that the final guide to Rossetti lies in her poetry. Certainly, there is power in the opening lines of her poem dedicated to one of her poetic mothers, Leticia Landon:

> Down-stairs I laugh, I sport and jest with all:
> But in my solitary room above
> I turn my face in silence to the wall;
> My heart is breaking for a little love. (L.E.L.)

Rossetti's faith was real, fervent and intense, even by Victorian standards. From as early as 1844, Rossetti attended Christ Church, Albany Street, whose minister, William Dodsworth, was a dedicated follower of the Tractarian movement (and who later converted to Roman Catholicism in 1851). Here she would not only have imbibed the centrality of the Eucharist for Christian faith but also been exposed to a vision of the liturgical year charged with meaning and power. The most transformational encounter came during Advent 1848. Rossetti heard the Apocalyptic sermons – 'The Signs of the Times' – preached at Christ Church, Albany Street, by Dodsworth. Their impact was such that the poet never lost that sense of wonder and the expectation of the Second Coming of Christ. Her 1893 commentary on the Apocalypse of John, *The Face of the Deep*, reflects the abiding impact of her early, formative experiences.

Running alongside her encounter with Dodsworth's sermons was another with John Keble's poetry and writing. In 1827, John Keble had published a book of poems which traced his devotional response to the liturgical year, *The Christian Year*. While William Michael claimed that his sister thought nothing of Keble as a poet, Christina's copy *The Christian Year* was heavily annotated and arguably taught her much about the way time and space can be constructed very differently from the mercantile, secular and consumerist world emerging in the nineteenth century. Though Rossetti's poetry outmatches Keble's verse at almost every point – contrast her poems for St Peter with his poems for St Peter in *The Christian Year* – she was surely influenced by Keble's 'poetry of reserve' which held that poetry was especially fit to speak of God, and, in essence, is the 'handmaid' of Christian belief.

A gift for simplicity, elusiveness and discretion may be, for Keble, a theological virtue, but it is a characteristic marker of much of Rossetti's best 'secular' poetry as much as her devotional verse. A poem like *Winter: My Secret*, included in her first major collection *Goblin Market and Other Poems*, arguably presents a repeated modus operandi for Rossetti, in which she eludes as she reveals, teasing her reader with promise and promise spurned:

> I tell my secret? No indeed, not I:
> Perhaps some day, who knows?
> But not today; it froze, and blows, and snows,
> And you're too curious: fie!
> You want to hear it? well:
> Only, my secret's mine, and I won't tell.

The promised (strip-)tease does not end there, but is reformulated and reconfigured:

> Suppose there is no secret after all
> [...]
> Perhaps my secret I may say,
> Or you may guess.

The secret could be many things – the writer's 'winter', her frigidity or virginity or the 'golden fruit' of fulfilment. If one is tempted by Theory again, it may be the writer's subjectivity, locked in by the 'I' which is performed at both the beginning and the end of the opening line. As the poem later claims, 'I wear my mask for warmth'. The speaker in the poem also wears 'a veil, a cloak, and other wraps'. Rossetti's speaker is then both allusive, elusive and fundamentally doubled – a mask wearer whose 'secret' seems to be structurally locked up.

In this mode, Rossetti is almost disconcertingly contemporary; disconcerting because she embodies a kind of tantalising confessional mode that has (with considerably less success) marked out a fair deal of contemporary poetry. In Rossetti's hands, however, the confessional remains always slightly out of sight. She models flagrant reserve. The notion of confessional, of course, has both a religious and a poetic connotation. The Latin root, *confiteri*, has implications of acknowledgement, especially acknowledgement together with another. In its early religious senses, it referred to martyrs who acknowledged, held to and admitted to their faith in the face of persecution or danger. It is a making public of a private truth, belief or fact.

Insofar as Rossetti operates in confessional mode, she does so with a teasing, tempting playfulness. Thus, in *The Heart Knoweth Its Own Bitterness*, she writes:

> To give, to give, not to receive,
>   I long to pour myself, my soul,
> Not to keep back or count or leave
>   But king with king to give the whole:
> I long for one to stir my deep –
>   I have had enough of help and gift –
>   I long for one to search and sift
> Myself, to take myself and keep.

There is a potent longing in these lines, a desire to both give and receive (with all of the religious and sexual connotations that has); there is an acknowledgement of desire and yet it is not clear that Rossetti ever quite expects to be in a position to 'let go' and be ravished, at least in this life.

Rossetti's ability to be discrete in a paradoxically garrulous way saves her from stumbling into that habit which can poison the most talented poet: earnestness. It is always a risk of those who are religious and, perhaps, in some of the later poems she cannot quite resist it enough. However, there is surely, in both her early and later work, a suppleness and simplicity which even in those poems can feel most familiar, as with *A Christmas Carol* – which is quite ravishing:

In the bleak mid-winter,
  Frosty wind made moan,
Earth stood hard as iron,
  Water like a stone;
Snow had fallen, snow on snow,
  Snow on snow,
In the bleak mid-winter,
  Long ago.

Of course, this capacity for ravishment is also found in occasional, quite devastating flourishes of excess. The poem *Goblin Market* has rightly been lauded, not only for its thematic richness, but its capacity to generate critical and sensuous pleasure. Notably, Rossetti herself indicated that the poem should be read as a children's fable – and, indeed, her gift for the childlike simplicity of nursery rhyme is shown in 1872's *Sing-Song: A Nursery Rhyme Book* – but *Goblin Market* very clearly indicates how poems can escape the stated intention of the poet. It is a poem which affords a plethora of critical readings, from creative accounts of the Eucharist, lesbian love, through to economic and sociological readings. It is also a poem with an exceptionally modern approach to line and rhythm, in which dactylic metre jostles with iambic. Indeed, John Ruskin's comment on the poem in 1861 (having been shown it by Dante Gabriel) was that it would never get published because of its 'irregular metre ... the calamity of modern poetry'. Whatever else it is, *Goblin Market*'s story of two women, Lizzie and Laura tempted by the 'fruits' of goblin-men is mouth-watering:

Morning and evening
Maids heard the goblins cry:
'Come buy our orchard fruits,
Come buy, come buy:
Apples and quinces,

Lemons and oranges,
Plump unpecked cherries,
Melons and raspberries,
Bloom-down-cheeked peaches,
Swart-headed mulberries,
Wild free-born cranberries,
Crab-apples, dewberries,
Pine-apples, blackberries,
Apricots, strawberries; –
All ripe together
In summer weather, –
Morns that pass by,
Fair eves that fly;
Come buy, come buy …'

Christina Rossetti's reputation has gone through a number of iterations. Leaving the visionary Ford Madox Ford's claims aside, Diane D'Amico suggests that, at the turn of the twentieth century, Rossetti was seen as a writer whose poetry revealed the invisible world of her faith; however, by the 1990s, Rossetti was read 'as a highly intelligent woman in a patriarchal society whose poetry reveals both victimisation and subversive feminism'.[3] Writing at the turn of the millennium, Cynthia Scheinberg suggests that, typically, feminist analyses of Victorian poets assume that 'women writers who actively supported religious institutions and affiliations were necessarily didactic, submissive, unenlightened, and uncreative reproducers of male religious hierarchy'.[4] There may be strong

3 Diane D'Amico, *Christina Rossetti: Faith, Gender, and Time* (Baton Rouge: Louisiana State University Press, 1999), p. 1.

4 Cynthia Scheinberg, *Women's Poetry and Religion in Victorian England: Jewish Identity and Christian Culture* (Cambridge: Cambridge University Press, 2002), p. 9.

evidence for that. Outside of her work as a poet, Christina and her sister Maria were involved in the *St Mary Magdalene Home for Fallen Women* in Highgate. The very idea of 'saving' women from 'fallenness' may strike post-modern sensibilities as a token of patriarchal ideas about gender and sexuality.

Rossetti's social, cultural and political 'time', of course, was one in which the mercantile and the mechanical was the emergent king. In Victorian times, the pressure was on to make and sell things as quickly as possible; this was the age of high-speed movement symbolised by the triumph of the train. By the time, Rossetti died in 1894, the telegraph, telephone and the combustion engine were beginning to reshape time yet again. The world had become small and humanity's place within it – knocked by emergent evolutionary ideas and often read as part of a mechanical, manufacturing process – seemed to be becoming very insignificant. Identity was increasingly being defined by mass production and mass consumption. Mass production techniques made cheapish but well-made consumer goods available to the British middle-classes for the first time; Rossetti's refrain in *Goblin Market* – 'Come buy, Come buy!' – echoed around middle-class lives (and increasingly working-class ones too) like never before.

Through this prism it may seem that Rossetti's turn, later in life, ever more towards the devotional and religious represents a reactionary, retrograde turn. Certainly, her late obsessions with the Second Coming of Christ and exclusive focus on devotional poetry may strike many as reactionary and lacking in the suppleness of her early work. However, that is a little unfair. In her 1857 poem, *A Better Resurrection*, she writes:

I have no wit, no words, no tears;
        My heart within me like a stone
Is numbed too much for hopes or fears;
        Look right, look left, I dwell alone;

I lift mine eyes, but dimmed with grief
No everlasting hills I see;
My life is in the falling leaf:
O Jesus, quicken me.

Her handling of religious desire in this early poem certainly has a tenderness and intimacy that is lacking in a later poem, like *Vigil of the Presentation*:

Long and dark the nights, dim and short the days,
Mounting weary heights on our weary ways,
Thee our God we praise.
Scaling heavenly heights by unearthly ways,
Thee our God we praise all our nights and days,
Thee our God we praise.

However, the shift from first-person singular to first-person plural is not necessarily a signal of failure or decay. It signals a shift in intention and a concentration on community a little alien to our fetishisation of the individual.

Nonetheless, to return to Sisson and Madox Ford at the close: if my gloss, 'Christina Rossetti is the great naked Victorian poet', is to have real traction, there is simply no doubt that it finds its grip in those magnificent intimacies of her earlier phases of writing. With perhaps the exception of Emily Dickinson, no one else has quite defined the power of the personal and the elusive in poetry. Certainly no one quite rivals her capacity to generate almost simultaneous reserve and excess. Rossetti's reputation is now secure, and part of what secures it is the way her finest poems create unequalled effects of intimacy that keeps her readers at a distance just at the moment they feel invited in.

NEW SELECTED POEMS

Goblin Market and Other Poems (1862)

GOBLIN MARKET

Morning and evening
Maids heard the goblins cry:
'Come buy our orchard fruits,
Come buy, come buy:
Apples and quinces,
Lemons and oranges,
Plump unpecked cherries,
Melons and raspberries,
Bloom-down-cheeked peaches,
Swart-headed mulberries,
Wild free-born cranberries,
Crab-apples, dewberries,
Pine-apples, blackberries,
Apricots, strawberries; –
All ripe together
In summer weather, –
Morns that pass by,
Fair eves that fly;
Come buy, come buy:
Our grapes fresh from the vine,
Pomegranates full and fine,
Dates and sharp bullaces,
Rare pears and greengages,
Damsons and bilberries,
Taste them and try:
Currants and gooseberries,
Bright-fire-like barberries,
Figs to fill your mouth,
Citrons from the South,

Sweet to tongue and sound to eye;
Come buy, come buy.'

Evening by evening
Among the brookside rushes,
Laura bowed her head to hear,
Lizzie veiled her blushes:
Crouching close together
In the cooling weather,
With clasping arms and cautioning lips,
With tingling cheeks and finger tips.
'Lie close,' Laura said,
Pricking up her golden head:
'We must not look at goblin men,
We must not buy their fruits:
Who knows upon what soil they fed
Their hungry thirsty roots?'
'Come buy,' call the goblins
Hobbling down the glen.
'Oh,' cried Lizzie, 'Laura, Laura,
You should not peep at goblin men.'
Lizzie covered up her eyes,
Covered close lest they should look;
Laura reared her glossy head,
And whispered like the restless brook:
'Look, Lizzie, look, Lizzie,
Down the glen tramp little men.
One hauls a basket,
One bears a plate,
One lugs a golden dish
Of many pounds weight.
How fair the vine must grow
Whose grapes are so luscious;
How warm the wind must blow

Through those fruit bushes.'
'No,' said Lizzie, 'No, no, no;
Their offers should not charm us,
Their evil gifts would harm us.'
She thrust a dimpled finger
In each ear, shut eyes and ran:
Curious Laura chose to linger
Wondering at each merchant man.
One had a cat's face,
One whisked a tail,
One tramped at a rat's pace,
One crawled like a snail,
One like a wombat prowled obtuse and furry,
One like a ratel tumbled hurry skurry.
She heard a voice like voice of doves
Cooing all together:
They sounded kind and full of loves
In the pleasant weather.

Laura stretched her gleaming neck
Like a rush-imbedded swan,
Like a lily from the beck,
Like a moonlit poplar branch,
Like a vessel at the launch
When its last restraint is gone.

Backwards up the mossy glen
Turned and trooped the goblin men,
With their shrill repeated cry,
'Come buy, come buy.'
When they reached where Laura was
They stood stock still upon the moss,
Leering at each other,
Brother with queer brother;

Signalling each other,
Brother with sly brother.
One set his basket down,
One reared his plate;
One began to weave a crown
Of tendrils, leaves, and rough nuts brown
(Men sell not such in any town);
One heaved the golden weight
Of dish and fruit to offer her:
'Come buy, come buy,' was still their cry.
Laura stared but did not stir,
Longed but had no money:
The whisk-tailed merchant bade her taste
In tones as smooth as honey,
The cat-faced purred,
The rat-faced spoke a word
Of welcome, and the snail-paced even was heard;
One parrot-voiced and jolly
Cried 'Pretty Goblin' still for 'Pretty Polly;' –
One whistled like a bird.

But sweet-tooth Laura spoke in haste:
'Good folk, I have no coin;
To take were to purloin:
I have no copper in my purse,
I have no silver either,
And all my gold is on the furze
That shakes in windy weather
Above the rusty heather.'
'You have much gold upon your head,'
They answered all together:
'Buy from us with a golden curl.'
She clipped a precious golden lock,
She dropped a tear more rare than pearl,

Then sucked their fruit globes fair or red:
Sweeter than honey from the rock,
Stronger than man-rejoicing wine,
Clearer than water flowed that juice;
She never tasted such before,
How should it cloy with length of use?
She sucked and sucked and sucked the more
Fruits which that unknown orchard bore;
She sucked until her lips were sore;
Then flung the emptied rinds away
But gathered up one kernel stone,
And knew not was it night or day
As she turned home alone.

Lizzie met her at the gate
Full of wise upbraidings:
'Dear, you should not stay so late,
Twilight is not good for maidens;
Should not loiter in the glen
In the haunts of goblin men.
Do you not remember Jeanie,
How she met them in the moonlight,
Took their gifts both choice and many,
Ate their fruits and wore their flowers
Plucked from bowers
Where summer ripens at all hours?
But ever in the noonlight
She pined and pined away;
Sought them by night and day,
Found them no more, but dwindled and grew grey;
Then fell with the first snow,
While to this day no grass will grow
Where she lies low:
I planted daisies there a year ago

That never blow.
You should not loiter so.'
'Nay, hush,' said Laura:
'Nay, hush, my sister:
I ate and ate my fill,
Yet my mouth waters still;
To-morrow night I will
Buy more;' and kissed her:
'Have done with sorrow;
I'll bring you plums tomorrow
Fresh on their mother twigs,
Cherries worth getting;
You cannot think what figs
My teeth have met in,
What melons icy-cold
Piled on a dish of gold
Too huge for me to hold,
What peaches with a velvet nap,
Pellucid grapes without one seed:
Odorous indeed must be the mead
Whereon they grow, and pure the wave they drink
With lilies at the brink,
And sugar-sweet their sap.'

Golden head by golden head,
Like two pigeons in one nest
Folded in each other's wings,
They lay down in their curtained bed:
Like two blossoms on one stem,
Like two flakes of new-fall'n snow,
Like two wands of ivory
Tipped with gold for awful kings.
Moon and stars gazed in at them,
Wind sang to them lullaby,

Lumbering owls forbore to fly,
Not a bat flapped to and fro
Round their rest:
Cheek to cheek and breast to breast
Locked together in one nest.

Early in the morning
When the first cock crowed his warning,
Neat like bees, as sweet and busy,
Laura rose with Lizzie:
Fetched in honey, milked the cows,
Aired and set to rights the house,
Kneaded cakes of whitest wheat,
Cakes for dainty mouths to eat,
Next churned butter, whipped up cream,
Fed their poultry, sat and sewed;
Talked as modest maidens should:
Lizzie with an open heart,
Laura in an absent dream,
One content, one sick in part;
One warbling for the mere bright day's delight,
One longing for the night.

At length slow evening came:
They went with pitchers to the reedy brook;
Lizzie most placid in her look,
Laura most like a leaping flame.
They drew the gurgling water from its deep;
Lizzie plucked purple and rich golden flags,
Then turning homeward said: 'The sunset flushes
Those furthest loftiest crags;
Come, Laura, not another maiden lags.
No wilful squirrel wags,
The beasts and birds are fast asleep.'

But Laura loitered still among the rushes
And said the bank was steep.

And said the hour was early still
The dew not fall'n, the wind not chill;
Listening ever, but not catching
The customary cry,
'Come buy, come buy,'
With its iterated jingle
Of sugar-baited words:
Not for all her watching
Once discerning even one goblin
Racing, whisking, tumbling, hobbling;
Let alone the herds
That used to tramp along the glen,
In groups or single,
Of brisk fruit-merchant men.
Till Lizzie urged, 'O Laura, come;
I hear the fruit-call but I dare not look:
You should not loiter longer at this brook:
Come with me home.
The stars rise, the moon bends her arc,
Each glowworm winks her spark,
Let us get home before the night grows dark:
For clouds may gather
Though this is summer weather,
Put out the lights and drench us through;
Then if we lost our way what should we do?'

Laura turned cold as stone
To find her sister heard that cry alone,
That goblin cry,
'Come buy our fruits, come buy.'
Must she then buy no more such dainty fruit?

Must she no more such succous pasture find,
Gone deaf and blind?
Her tree of life drooped from the root:
She said not one word in her heart's sore ache;
But peering thro' the dimness, nought discerning,
Trudged home, her pitcher dripping all the way;
So crept to bed, and lay
Silent till Lizzie slept;
Then sat up in a passionate yearning,
And gnashed her teeth for baulked desire, and wept
As if her heart would break.

Day after day, night after night,
Laura kept watch in vain
In sullen silence of exceeding pain.
She never caught again the goblin cry:
'Come buy, come buy;' –
She never spied the goblin men
Hawking their fruits along the glen:
But when the noon waxed bright
Her hair grew thin and grey;
She dwindled, as the fair full moon doth turn
To swift decay and burn
Her fire away.

One day remembering her kernel-stone
She set it by a wall that faced the south;
Dewed it with tears, hoped for a root,
Watched for a waxing shoot,
But there came none;
It never saw the sun,
It never felt the trickling moisture run:
While with sunk eyes and faded mouth
She dreamed of melons, as a traveller sees

False waves in desert drouth
With shade of leaf-crowned trees,
And burns the thirstier in the sandful breeze.

She no more swept the house,
Tended the fowls or cows,
Fetched honey, kneaded cakes of wheat,
Brought water from the brook:
But sat down listless in the chimney-nook
And would not eat.

Tender Lizzie could not bear
To watch her sister's cankerous care
Yet not to share.
She night and morning
Caught the goblins' cry:
'Come buy our orchard fruits,
Come buy, come buy;' –
Beside the brook, along the glen,
She heard the tramp of goblin men,
The yoke and stir
Poor Laura could not hear;
Longed to buy fruit to comfort her,
But feared to pay too dear.
She thought of Jeanie in her grave,
Who should have been a bride;
But who for joys brides hope to have
Fell sick and died
In her gay prime,
In earliest winter time
With the first glazing rime,
With the first snow-fall of crisp winter time.

Till Laura dwindling
Seemed knocking at Death's door:
Then Lizzie weighed no more
Better and worse;
But put a silver penny in her purse,
Kissed Laura, crossed the heath with clumps of furze
At twilight, halted by the brook:
And for the first time in her life
Began to listen and look.

Laughed every goblin
When they spied her peeping:
Came towards her hobbling,
Flying, running, leaping,
Puffing and blowing,
Chuckling, clapping, crowing,
Clucking and gobbling,
Mopping and mowing,
Full of airs and graces,
Pulling wry faces,
Demure grimaces,
Cat-like and rat-like,
Ratel- and wombat-like,
Snail-paced in a hurry,
Parrot-voiced and whistler,
Helter skelter, hurry skurry,
Chattering like magpies,
Fluttering like pigeons,
Gliding like fishes, –
Hugged her and kissed her:
Squeezed and caressed her:
Stretched up their dishes,
Panniers, and plates:
'Look at our apples

Russet and dun,
Bob at our cherries,
Bite at our peaches,
Citrons and dates,
Grapes for the asking,
Pears red with basking
Out in the sun,
Plums on their twigs;
Pluck them and suck them,
Pomegranates, figs.' –

'Good folk,' said Lizzie,
Mindful of Jeanie:
'Give me much and many: –
Held out her apron,
Tossed them her penny.
'Nay, take a seat with us,
Honour and eat with us,'
They answered grinning:
'Our feast is but beginning.
Night yet is early,
Warm and dew-pearly,
Wakeful and starry:
Such fruits as these
No man can carry:
Half their bloom would fly,
Half their dew would dry,
Half their flavour would pass by.
Sit down and feast with us,
Be welcome guest with us,
Cheer you and rest with us.' –
'Thank you,' said Lizzie: 'But one waits
At home alone for me:
So without further parleying,

If you will not sell me any
Of your fruits though much and many,
Give me back my silver penny
I tossed you for a fee.' –
They began to scratch their pates,
No longer wagging, purring,
But visibly demurring,
Grunting and snarling.
One called her proud,
Cross-grained, uncivil;
Their tones waxed loud,
Their looks were evil.
Lashing their tails
They trod and hustled her,
Elbowed and jostled her,
Clawed with their nails,
Barking, mewing, hissing, mocking,
Tore her gown and soiled her stocking,
Twitched her hair out by the roots,
Stamped upon her tender feet,
Held her hands and squeezed their fruits
Against her mouth to make her eat.
White and golden Lizzie stood,
Like a lily in a flood, –
Like a rock of blue-veined stone
Lashed by tides obstreperously, –
Like a beacon left alone
In a hoary roaring sea,
Sending up a golden fire, –
Like a fruit-crowned orange-tree
White with blossoms honey-sweet
Sore beset by wasp and bee, –
Like a royal virgin town
Topped with gilded dome and spire

Close beleaguered by a fleet
Mad to tug her standard down.

One may lead a horse to water,
Twenty cannot make him drink.
Though the goblins cuffed and caught her,
Coaxed and fought her,
Bullied and besought her,
Scratched her, pinched her black as ink,
Kicked and knocked her,
Mauled and mocked her,
Lizzie uttered not a word;
Would not open lip from lip
Lest they should cram a mouthful in:
But laughed in heart to feel the drip
Of juice that syrupped all her face,
And lodged in dimples of her chin,
And streaked her neck which quaked like curd.
At last the evil people,
Worn out by her resistance,
Flung back her penny, kicked their fruit
Along whichever road they took,
Not leaving root or stone or shoot;
Some writhed into the ground,
Some dived into the brook
With ring and ripple,
Some scudded on the gale without a sound,
Some vanished in the distance.

In a smart, ache, tingle,
Lizzie went her way;
Knew not was it night or day;
Sprang up the bank, tore thro' the furze,
Threaded copse and dingle,

And heard her penny jingle
Bouncing in her purse, –
Its bounce was music to her ear.
She ran and ran
As if she feared some goblin man
Dogged her with gibe or curse
Or something worse:
But not one goblin scurried after,
Nor was she pricked by fear;
The kind heart made her windy-paced
That urged her home quite out of breath with haste
And inward laughter.

She cried, 'Laura,' up the garden,
'Did you miss me?
Come and kiss me.
Never mind my bruises,
Hug me, kiss me, suck my juices
Squeezed from goblin fruits for you,
Goblin pulp and goblin dew.
Eat me, drink me, love me;
Laura, make much of me;
For your sake I have braved the glen
And had to do with goblin merchant men.'

Laura started from her chair,
Flung her arms up in the air,
Clutched her hair:
'Lizzie, Lizzie, have you tasted
For my sake the fruit forbidden?
Must your light like mine be hidden,
Your young life like mine be wasted,
Undone in mine undoing,
And ruined in my ruin,

Thirsty, cankered, goblin-ridden?' –
She clung about her sister,
Kissed and kissed and kissed her:
Tears once again
Refreshed her shrunken eyes,
Dropping like rain
After long sultry drouth;
Shaking with aguish fear, and pain,
She kissed and kissed her with a hungry mouth.

Her lips began to scorch,
That juice was wormwood to her tongue,
She loathed the feast:
Writhing as one possessed she leaped and sung,
Rent all her robe, and wrung
Her hands in lamentable haste,
And beat her breast.
Her locks streamed like the torch
Borne by a racer at full speed,
Or like the mane of horses in their flight,
Or like an eagle when she stems the light
Straight toward the sun,
Or like a caged thing freed,
Or like a flying flag when armies run.

Swift fire spread through her veins, knocked at her heart,
Met the fire smouldering there
And overbore its lesser flame;
She gorged on bitterness without a name:
Ah! fool, to choose such part
Of soul-consuming care!
Sense failed in the mortal strife:
Like the watch-tower of a town
Which an earthquake shatters down,

Like a lightning-stricken mast,
Like a wind-uprooted tree
Spun about,
Like a foam-topped waterspout
Cast down headlong in the sea,
She fell at last;
Pleasure past and anguish past,
Is it death or is it life?

Life out of death.
That night long Lizzie watched by her,
Counted her pulse's flagging stir,
Felt for her breath,
Held water to her lips, and cooled her face
With tears and fanning leaves:
But when the first birds chirped about their eaves,
And early reapers plodded to the place
Of golden sheaves,
And dew-wet grass
Bowed in the morning winds so brisk to pass,
And new buds with new day
Opened of cup-like lilies on the stream,
Laura awoke as from a dream,
Laughed in the innocent old way,
Hugged Lizzie but not twice or thrice;
Her gleaming locks showed not one thread of grey,
Her breath was sweet as May
And light danced in her eyes.

Days, weeks, months, years
Afterwards, when both were wives
With children of their own;
Their mother-hearts beset with fears,
Their lives bound up in tender lives;

Laura would call the little ones
And tell them of her early prime,
Those pleasant days long gone
Of not-returning time:
Would talk about the haunted glen,
The wicked, quaint fruit-merchant men,
Their fruits like honey to the throat
But poison in the blood;
(Men sell not such in any town):
Would tell them how her sister stood
In deadly peril to do her good,
And win the fiery antidote:
Then joining hands to little hands
Would bid them cling together,
'For there is no friend like a sister
In calm or stormy weather;
To cheer one on the tedious way,
To fetch one if one goes astray,
To lift one if one totters down,
To strengthen whilst one stands.'

IN THE ROUND TOWER AT JHANSI

8 June 1857

A hundred, a thousand to one; even so;
  Not a hope in the world remained:
The swarming howling wretches below
  Gained and gained and gained.

Skene looked at his pale young wife: –
  'Is the time come?' – 'The time is come!' –
Young, strong, and so full of life:
  The agony struck them dumb.

Close his arm about her now,
  Close her cheek to his,
Close the pistol to her brow –
  God forgive them this!

'Will it hurt much?' – 'No, mine own:
  I wish I could bear the pang for both.'
'I wish I could bear the pang alone:
  Courage, dear, I am not loth.'

Kiss and kiss: 'It is not pain
  Thus to kiss and die.
One kiss more.' – 'And yet one again.' –
  'Good-bye.' – 'Good-bye.'

DREAM-LAND

Where sunless rivers weep
Their waves into the deep,
She sleeps a charméd sleep:
Awake her not.
Led by a single star,
She came from very far
To seek where shadows are
Her pleasant lot.

She left the rosy morn,
She left the fields of corn,
For twilight cold and lorn
And water springs.
Thro' sleep, as thro' a veil,
She sees the sky look pale,
And hears the nightingale
That sadly sings.

Rest, rest, a perfect rest
Shed over brow and breast;
Her face is toward the west,
The purple land.
She cannot see the grain
Ripening on hill and plain;
She cannot feel the rain
Upon her hand.

Rest, rest, for evermore
Upon a mossy shore;
Rest, rest at the heart's core
Till time shall cease:
Sleep that no pain shall wake;
Night that no morn shall break,
Till joy shall overtake
Her perfect peace.

AT HOME

When I was dead, my spirit turned
    To seek the much-frequented house:
I passed the door, and saw my friends
    Feasting beneath green orange boughs;
From hand to hand they pushed the wine,
    They sucked the pulp of plum and peach;
They sang, they jested, and they laughed,
    For each was loved of each.

I listened to their honest chat:
    Said one: 'Tomorrow we shall be
Plod plod along the featureless sands,
    And coasting miles and miles of sea.'
Said one: 'Before the turn of tide
    We will achieve the eyrie-seat.'
Said one: 'Tomorrow shall be like
    Today, but much more sweet.'

'Tomorrow,' said they, strong with hope,
    And dwelt upon the pleasant way:
'Tomorrow,' cried they, one and all,
    While no one spoke of yesterday.
Their life stood full at blessed noon;
    I, only I, had passed away:
'Tomorrow and today,' they cried;
    I was of yesterday.

I shivered comfortless, but cast
No chill across the tablecloth;
I, all-forgotten, shivered, sad
To stay, and yet to part how loth:
I passed from the familiar room,
I who from love had passed away,
Like the remembrance of a guest
That tarrieth but a day.

LOVE FROM THE NORTH

I had a love in soft south land,
  Beloved thro' April far in May;
He waited on my lightest breath,
  And never dared to say me nay.

He saddened if my cheer was sad,
  But gay he grew if I was gay;
We never differed on a hair,
  My yes his yes, my nay his nay.

The wedding hour was come, the aisles
  Were flushed with sun and flowers that day;
I pacing balanced in my thoughts, –
  'It's quite too late to think of nay.' –

My bridegroom answered in his turn,
  Myself had almost answered 'yea':
When thro' the flashing nave I heard.
  A struggle and resounding 'nay.'

Bridesmaids and bridegroom shrank in fear,
  But I stood high who stood at bay:
'And if I answer yea, fair Sir,
  What man art thou to bar with nay?'

He was a strong man from the north,
  Light-locked, with eyes of dangerous gray:
'Put yea by for another time
  In which I will not say thee nay.'

He took me in his strong white arms,
He bore me on his horse away
O'er crag, morass, and hair-breadth pass,
But never asked me yea or nay.

He made me fast with book and bell,
With links of love he makes me stay;
Till now I've neither heart nor power
Nor will nor wish to say him nay.

WINTER RAIN

Every valley drinks,
  Every dell and hollow:
Where the kind rain sinks and sinks,
  Green of Spring will follow.

Yet a lapse of weeks
  Buds will burst their edges,
Strip their wool-coats, glue-coats, streaks,
  In the woods and hedges;

Weave a bower of love
  For birds to meet each other,
Weave a canopy above
  Nest and egg and mother.

But for fattening rain
  We should have no flowers,
Never a bud or leaf again
  But for soaking showers;

Never a mated bird
  In the rocking tree-tops,
Never indeed a flock or herd
  To graze upon the lea-crops.

Lambs so woolly white,
  Sheep the sun-bright leas on,
They could have no grass to bite
  But for rain in season.

We should find no moss
  In the shadiest places,
Find no waving meadow grass
  Pied with broad-eyed daisies:

But miles of barren sand,
  With never a son or daughter,
Not a lily on the land,
  Or lily on the water.

COUSIN KATE

I was a cottage maiden
  Hardened by sun and air,
Contented with my cottage mates,
  Not mindful I was fair.
Why did a great lord find me out,
  And praise my flaxen hair?
Why did a great lord find me out
  To fill my heart with care?

He lured me to his palace home –
  Woe's me for joy thereof –
To lead a shameless shameful life,
  His plaything and his love.
He wore me like a silken knot,
  He changed me like a glove;
So now I moan, an unclean thing,
  Who might have been a dove.

O Lady Kate, my cousin Kate,
  You grew more fair than I:
He saw you at your father's gate,
  Chose you, and cast me by.
He watched your steps along the lane,
  Your work among the rye;
He lifted you from mean estate
  To sit with him on high.

Because you were so good and pure
  He bound you with his ring:
The neighbours call you good and pure,
  Call me an outcast thing.
Even so I sit and howl in dust,
  You sit in gold and sing:
Now which of us has tenderer heart?
  You had the stronger wing.

O cousin Kate, my love was true,
  Your love was writ in sand:
If he had fooled not me but you,
  If you stood where I stand,
Heed not have won me with his love
  Nor bought me with his land;
I would have spit into his face
  And not have taken his hand.

Yet I've a gift you have not got,
  And seem not like to get:
For all your clothes and wedding-ring
  I've little doubt you fret.
My fair-haired son, my shame, my pride,
  Cling closer, closer yet:
Your father would give lands for one
  To wear his coronet.

THE LAMBS OF GRASMERE (1860)

The upland flocks grew starved and thinned;
  Their shepherds scarce could feed the lambs
Whose milkless mothers butted them,
  Or who were orphaned of their dams.
The lambs athirst for mother's milk
  Filled all the place with piteous sounds:
Their mothers' bones made white for miles
  The pastureless wet pasture grounds.

Day after day, night after night,
  From lamb to lamb the shepherds went,
With teapots for the bleating mouths
  Instead of nature's nourishment.
The little shivering gaping things
  Soon knew the step that brought them aid,
And fondled the protecting hand,
  And rubbed it with a woolly head.

Then, as the days waxed on to weeks,
  It was a pretty sight to see
These lambs with frisky heads and tails
  Skipping and leaping on the lea,
Bleating in tender, trustful tones,
  Resting on rocky crag or mound,
And following the beloved feet
  That once had sought for them and found.

These very shepherds of their flocks,
   These loving lambs so meek to please,
Are worthy of recording words
   And honour in their due degrees:
So I might live a hundred years,
   And roam from strand to foreign strand,
Yet not forget this flooded spring
   And scarce-saved lambs of Westmoreland.

A BIRTHDAY

My heart is like a singing bird
  Whose nest is in a watered shoot;
My heart is like an apple-tree
  Whose boughs are bent with thickset fruit;
My heart is like a rainbow shell
  That paddles in a halcyon sea;
My heart is gladder than all these
  Because my love is come to me.

Raise me a dais of silk and down;
  Hang it with vair and purple dyes;
Carve it in doves and pomegranates,
  And peacocks with a hundred eyes;
Work it in gold and silver grapes,
  In leaves and silver fleurs-de-lys;
Because the birthday of my life
  Is come, my love is come to me.

REMEMBER

Remember me when I am gone away,
   Gone far away into the silent land;
   When you can no more hold me by the hand,
Nor I half turn to go yet turning stay.
Remember me when no more day by day
   You tell me of our future that you planned:
Only remember me; you understand
It will be late to counsel then or pray.
Yet if you should forget me for a while
   And afterwards remember, do not grieve:
   For if the darkness and corruption leave
   A vestige of the thoughts that once I had,
Better by far you should forget and smile
   Than that you should remember and be sad.

AFTER DEATH

The curtains were half drawn, the floor was swept
And strewn with rushes, rosemary and may
Lay thick upon the bed on which I lay,
Where thro' the lattice ivy-shadows crept.
He leaned above me, thinking that I slept
And could not hear him; but I heard him say:
'Poor child, poor child': and as he turned away
Came a deep silence, and I knew he wept.
He did not touch the shroud, or raise the fold
That hid my face, or take my hand in his,
Or ruffle the smooth pillows for my head:
He did not love me living; but once dead
He pitied me; and very sweet it is
To know he still is warm tho' I am cold.

AN APPLE-GATHERING

I plucked pink blossoms from mine apple tree
  And wore them all that evening in my hair:
Then in due season when I went to see
    I found no apples there.

With dangling basket all along the grass
  As I had come I went the selfsame track:
My neighbours mocked me while they saw me pass
    So empty-handed back.

Lilian and Lilias smiled in trudging by,
  Their heaped-up basket teazed me like a jeer;
Sweet-voiced they sang beneath the sunset sky,
    Their mother's home was near.

Plump Gertrude passed me with her basket full,
  A stronger hand than hers helped it along;
A voice talked with her thro' the shadows cool
    More sweet to me than song.

Ah Willie, Willie, was my love less worth
  Than apples with their green leaves piled above?
I counted rosiest apples on the earth
    Of far less worth than love.

So once it was with me you stooped to talk
  Laughing and listening in this very lane:
To think that by this way we used to walk
    We shall not walk again!

I let me neighbours pass me, ones and twos
  And groups; the latest said the night grew chill,
And hastened: but I loitered, while the dews
    Fell fast I loitered still.

ECHO

Come to me in the silence of the night;
  Come in the speaking silence of a dream;
Come with soft rounded cheeks and eyes as bright
  As sunlight on a stream;
    Come back in tears,
O memory, hope, love of finished years.

Oh dream how sweet, too sweet, too bitter sweet,
  Whose wakening should have been in Paradise,
Where souls brimfull of love abide and meet;
  Where thirsting longing eyes
    Watch the slow door
That opening, letting in, lets out no more.

Yet come to me in dreams, that I may live
  My very life again tho' cold in death:
Come back to me in dreams, that I may give
  Pulse for pulse, breath for breath:
    Speak low, lean low,
As long ago, my love, how long ago.

WINTER: MY SECRET

I tell my secret? No indeed, not I:
Perhaps some day, who knows?
But not today; it froze, and blows and snows,
And you're too curious: fie!
You want to hear it? well:
Only, my secret's mine, and I won't tell.

Or, after all, perhaps there's none:
Suppose there is no secret after all,
But only just my fun.
Today's a nipping day, a biting day;
In which one wants a shawl,
A veil, a cloak, and other wraps:
I cannot ope to everyone who taps,
And let the draughts come whistling thro' my hall;
Come bounding and surrounding me,
Come buffeting, astounding me,
Nipping and clipping thro' my wraps and all.
I wear my mask for warmth: who ever shows
His nose to Russian snows
To be pecked at by every wind that blows?
You would not peck? I thank you for good will,
Believe, but leave the truth untested still.

Spring's an expansive time: yet I don't trust
March with its peck of dust,
Nor April with its rainbow-crowned brief showers,
Nor even May, whose flowers
One frost may wither thro' the sunless hours.

Perhaps some languid summer day,
When drowsy birds sing less and less,
And golden fruit is ripening to excess,
If there's not too much sun nor too much cloud,
And the warm wind is neither still nor loud,
Perhaps my secret I may say,
Or you may guess.

ANOTHER SPRING

If I might see another Spring,
   Ied not plant summer flowers and wait:
Ied have my crocuses at once,
   My leafless pink mezereons,
My chill-veined snow-drops, choicer yet
   My white or azure violet,
Leaf-nested primrose; anything
      To blow at once, not late.

If I might see another Spring
   Ied listen to the daylight birds
That build their nests and pair and sing,
   Nor wait for mateless nightingale;
Ied listen to the lusty herds,
   The ewes with lambs as white as snow,
Ied find out music in the hail
      And all the winds that blow.

If I might see another Spring –
   Oh stinging comment on my past
That all my past results in 'if' –
   If I might see another Spring,
Ied laugh to-day, to-day is brief;
   I would not wait for anything:
Ied use to-day that cannot last,
      Be glad to-day and sing.

FATA MORGANA

A blue-eyed phantom far before
  Is laughing, leaping toward the sun:
Like lead I chase it evermore,
    I pant and run.

It breaks the sunlight bound on bound:
  Goes singing as it leaps along
To sheep-bells with a dreamy sound
    A dreamy song.

I laugh, it is so brisk and gay;
  It is so far before, I weep:
I hope I shall lie down some day,
    Lie down and sleep.

NO, THANK YOU, JOHN

I never said I loved you, John:
  Why will you teaze me, day by day,
And wax a weariness to think upon
    With always 'do' and 'pray'?

You know I never loved you, John;
  No fault of mine made me your toast:
Why will you haunt me with a face as wan
    As shows an hour-old ghost?

I dare say Meg or Moll would take
  Pity upon you, if youed ask:
And pray don't remain single for my sake
    Who can't perform that task.

I have no heart? – Perhaps I have not;
  But then you're mad to take offence
That I don't give you what I have not got:
    Use your common sense.

Let bygones be bygones:
  Don't call me false, who owed not to be true:
Ied rather answer 'No' to fifty Johns
    Than answer 'Yes' to you.

Let's mar our pleasant days no more,
  Song-birds of passage, days of youth:
Catch at today, forget the days before:
    I'll wink at your untruth.

Let us strike hands as hearty friends;
No more, no less: and friendship's good:
Only don't keep in view ulterior ends,
And points not understood

In open treaty. Rise above
Quibbles and shuffling off and on:
Here's friendship for you if you like; but love, –
No, thank you, John.

TWILIGHT CALM

Oh, pleasant eventide!
Clouds on the western side
Grow grey and greyer, hiding the warm sun:
The bees and birds, their happy labours done,
Seek their close nests and bide.

Screened in the leafy wood
The stock-doves sit and brood:
The very squirrel leaps from bough to bough
But lazily; pauses; and settles now
Where once he stored his food.

One by one the flowers close,
Lily and dewy rose
Shutting their tender petals from the moon:
The grasshoppers are still; but not so soon
Are still the noisy crows.

The dormouse squats and eats
Choice little dainty bits
Beneath the spreading roots of a broad lime;
Nibbling his fill he stops from time to time
And listens where he sits.

From far the lowings come
Of cattle driven home:
From farther still the wind brings fitfully
The vast continual murmur of the sea,
Now loud, now almost dumb.

The gnats whirl in the air,
The evening gnats; and there
The owl opes broad his eyes and wings to sail
For prey; the bat wakes; and the shell-less snail
Comes forth, clammy and bare.

Hark! that's the nightingale,
Telling the selfsame tale
Her song told when this ancient earth was young:
So echoes answered when her song was sung
In the first wooded vale.

We call it love and pain
The passion of her strain;
And yet we little understand or know:
Why should it not be rather joy that so
Throbs in each throbbing vein?

In separate herds the deer
Lie; here the bucks, and here
The does, and by its mother sleeps the fawn:
Through all the hours of night until the dawn
They sleep, forgetting fear.

The hare sleeps where it lies,
With wary half-closed eyes;
The cock has ceased to crow, the hen to cluck:
Only the fox is out, some heedless duck
Or chicken to surprise.

Remote, each single star
Comes out, till there they are
All shining brightly: how the dews fall damp!
While close at hand the glow-worm lights her lamp
Or twinkles from afar.

But evening now is done
As much as if the sun
Day-giving had arisen in the East:
For night has come; and the great calm has ceased,
The quiet sands have run.

WIFE TO HUSBAND

Pardon the faults in me,
   For the love of years ago:
      Goodbye.
I must drift across the sea,
   I must sink into the snow,
      I must die.

You can bask in this sun,
   You can drink wine, and eat:
      Goodbye.
I must gird myself and run,
   Tho' with unready feet:
      I must die.

Blank sea to sail upon,
   Cold bed to sleep in:
      Goodbye.
While you clasp, I must be gone
   For all your weeping:
      I must die.

A kiss for one friend,
   And a word for two, –
      Goodbye: –
A lock that you must send,
   A kindness you must do:
      I must die.

Not a word for you,
Not a lock or kiss,
Goodbye.
We, one, must part in two;
Verily death is this:
I must die.

SHUT OUT

The door was shut. I looked between
    Its iron bars; and saw it lie,
    My garden, mine, beneath the sky,
Pied with all flowers bedewed and green:

From bough to bough the song-birds crossed,
    From flower to flower the moths and bees;
    With all its nests and stately trees
It had been mine, and it was lost.

A shadowless spirit kept the gate,
    Blank and unchanging like the grave.
    I peering thro' said: 'Let me have
Some buds to cheer my outcast state.'

He answered not. 'Or give me, then,
    But one small twig from shrub or tree;
    And bid my home remember me
Until I come to it again.'

The spirit was silent; but he took
    Mortar and stone to build a wall;
    He left no loophole great or small
Thro' which my straining eyes might look:

So now I sit here quite alone
    Blinded with tears; nor grieve for that,
    For nought is left worth looking at
Since my delightful land is gone.

A violet bed is budding near,
    Wherein a lark has made her nest:
    And good they are, but not the best;
And dear they are, but not so dear.

SONG

When I am dead, my dearest,
 Sing no sad songs for me;
Plant thou no roses at my head,
 Nor shady cypress tree:
Be the green grass above me
 With showers and dewdrops wet;
And if thou wilt, remember,
 And if thou wilt, forget.

I shall not see the shadows,
 I shall not feel the rain;
I shall not hear the nightingale
 Sing on, as if in pain:
And dreaming through the twilight
 That doth not rise nor set,
Haply I may remember,
 And haply may forget.

BITTER FOR SWEET

Summer is gone with all its roses,
  Its sun and perfumes and sweet flowers,
Its warm air and refreshing showers:
    And even Autumn closes.

Yea, Autumn's chilly self is going,
  And winter comes which is yet colder;
Each day the hoar-frost waxes bolder,
    And the last buds cease blowing.

SISTER MAUDE

Who told my mother of my shame,
  Who told my father of my dear?
Oh who but Maude, my sister Maude,
  Who lurked to spy and peer.

Cold he lies, as cold as stone,
  With his clotted curls about his face:
The comeliest corpse in all the world
  And worthy of a queen's embrace.

You might have spared his soul, sister,
  Have spared my soul, your own soul too:
Though I had not been born at all,
  Heed never have looked at you.

My father may sleep in Paradise,
  My mother at Heaven-gate:
But sister Maude shall get no sleep
  Either early or late.

My father may wear a golden gown,
  My mother a crown may win;
If my dear and I knocked at Heaven-gate
  Perhaps theyed let us in:
But sister Maude, oh sister Maude,
  Bide *you* with death and sin.

THE FIRST SPRING DAY

I wonder if the sap is stirring yet,
If wintry birds are dreaming of a mate,
If frozen snowdrops feel as yet the sun
And crocus fires are kindling one by one:
        Sing, robin, sing;
I still am sore in doubt concerning Spring.

I wonder if the springtide of this year
Will bring another Spring both lost and dear;
If heart and spirit will find out their Spring,
Or if the world alone will bud and sing:
        Sing, hope, to me;
Sweet notes, my hope, soft notes for memory.

The sap will surely quicken soon or late,
The tardiest bird will twitter to a mate;
So Spring must dawn again with warmth and bloom,
Or in this world, or in the world to come:
        Sing, voice of Spring,
Till I too blossom and rejoice and sing.

THE CONVENT THRESHOLD

There's blood between us, love, my love,
There's father's blood, there's brother's blood;
And blood's a bar I cannot pass:
I choose the stairs that mount above,
Stair after golden skyward stair,
To city and to sea of glass.
My lily feet are soiled with mud,
With scarlet mud which tells a tale
Of hope that was, of guilt that was,
Of love that shall not yet avail;
Alas, my heart, if I could bare
My heart, this selfsame stain is there:
I seek the sea of glass and fire
To wash the spot, to burn the snare;
Lo, stairs are meant to lift us higher:
Mount with me, mount the kindled stair.

Your eyes look earthward, mine look up.
I see the far-off city grand,
Beyond the hills a watered land,
Beyond the gulf a gleaming strand
Of mansions where the righteous sup;
Who sleep at ease among their trees,
Or wake to sing a cadenced hymn
With Cherubim and Seraphim;
They bore the Cross, they drained the cup,
Racked, roasted, crushed, wrenched limb from limb,
They the offscouring of the world:
The heaven of starry heavens unfurled,
The sun before their face is dim.

You looking earthward, what see you?
Milk-white, wine-flushed among the vines,
Up and down leaping, to and fro,
Most glad, most full, made strong with wines,
Blooming as peaches pearled with dew,
Their golden windy hair afloat,
Love-music warbling in their throat,
Young men and women come and go.

You linger, yet the time is short:
Flee for your life, gird up your strength
To flee; the shadows stretched at length
Show that day wanes, that night draws nigh;
Flee to the mountain, tarry not.
Is this a time for smile and sigh,
For songs among the secret trees
Where sudden blue birds nest and sport?
The time is short and yet you stay:
Today, while it is called today,
Kneel, wrestle, knock, do violence, pray;
Today is short, tomorrow nigh:
Why will you die? why will you die?

You sinned with me a pleasant sin:
Repent with me, for I repent.
Woe's me the lore I must unlearn!
Woe's me that easy way we went,
So rugged when I would return!
How long until my sleep begin,
How long shall stretch these nights and days?
Surely, clean Angels cry, she prays;
She laves her soul with tedious tears:
How long must stretch these years and years?

I turn from you my cheeks and eyes,
My hair which you shall see no more –
Alas for joy that went before,
For joy that dies, for love that dies.
Only my lips still turn to you,
My livid lips that cry, Repent.
O weary life, O weary Lent,
O weary time whose stars are few.

How shall I rest in Paradise,
Or sit on steps of heaven alone?
If Saints and Angels spoke of love
Should I not answer from my throne:
Have pity upon me, ye my friends,
For I have heard the sound thereof:
Should I not turn with yearning eyes,
Turn earthwards with a pitiful pang?
Oh save me from a pang in heaven.
By all the gifts we took and gave,
Repent, repent, and be forgiven:
This life is long, but yet it ends;
Repent and purge your soul and save:
No gladder song the morning stars
Upon their birthday morning sang
Than Angels sing when one repents.

I tell you what I dreamed last night:
A spirit with transfigured face
Fire-footed clomb an infinite space.
I heard his hundred pinions clang,
Heaven-bells rejoicing rang and rang,
Heaven-air was thrilled with subtle scents,
Worlds spun upon their rushing cars.
He mounted, shrieking, 'Give me light!'

Still light was poured on him, more light;
Angels, Archangels he outstripped
Exulting in exceeding might,
And trod the skirts of Cherubim.
Still 'Give me light,' he shrieked; and dipped
His thirsty face, and drank a sea,
Athirst with thirst it could not slake.
I saw him, drunk with knowledge, take
From aching brows the aureole crown –
His locks writhe like a cloven snake –
He left his throne to grovel down
And lick the dust of Seraphs' feet:
For what is knowledge duly weighed?
Knowledge is strong, but love is sweet;
Yea, all the progress he had made
Was but to learn that all is small
Save love, for love is all in all.

I tell you what I dreamed last night:
It was not dark, it was not light,
Cold dews had drenched my plenteous hair
Through clay; you came to seek me there.
And 'Do you dream of me?' you said.
My heart was dust that used to leap
To you; I answered half asleep:
'My pillow is damp, my sheets are red,
There's a leaden tester to my bed:
Find you a warmer playfellow
A warmer pillow for your head,
A kinder love to love than mine.'
You wrung your hands, while I, like lead
Crushed downwards through the sodden earth;
You smote your hands but not in mirth,
And reeled but were not drunk with wine.

For all night long I dreamed of you;
I woke and prayed against my will,
Then slept to dream of you again.
At length I rose and knelt and prayed.
I cannot write the words I said,
My words were slow, my tears were few;
But through the dark my silence spoke
Like thunder. When this morning broke,
My face was pinched, my hair was grey,
And frozen blood was on the sill
Where stifling in my struggle I lay.

If now you saw me you would say:
Where is the face I used to love?
And I would answer: Gone before;
It tarries veiled in paradise.
When once the morning star shall rise,
When earth with shadow flees away
And we stand safe within the door,
Then you shall lift the veil thereof.
Look up, rise up: for far above
Our palms are grown, our place is set;
There we shall meet as once we met
And love with old familiar love.

UP-HILL

Does the road wind up-hill all the way?
  Yes, to the very end.
Will the day's journey take the whole long day?
  From morn to night, my friend.

But is there for the night a resting-place?
  A roof for when the slow dark hours begin.
May not the darkness hide it from my face?
  You cannot miss that inn.

Shall I meet other wayfarers at night?
  Those who have gone before.
Then must I knock, or call when just in sight?
  They will not keep you standing at that door.

Shall I find comfort, travel-sore and weak?
  Of labour you shall find the sum.
Will there be beds for me and all who seek?
  Yea, beds for all who come.

‘A BRUISED REED SHALL HE NOT BREAK’

I will accept thy will to do and be,
 Thy hatred and intolerance of sin,
 Thy will at least to love, that burns within
  And thirsteth after Me:
So will I render fruitful, blessing still
 The germs and small beginnings in thy heart,
 Because thy will cleaves to the better part. –
  Alas, I cannot will.

Dost not thou will, poor soul? Yet I receive
 The inner unseen longings of the soul,
 I guide them turning towards Me; I control
  And charm hearts till they grieve:
If thou desire, it yet shall come to pass,
 Tho' thou but wish indeed to choose My love;
 For I have power in earth and heaven above. –
  I cannot wish, alas!

What, neither choose nor wish to choose? and yet
 I still must strive to win thee and constrain:
 For thee I hung upon the cross in pain,
  How then can I forget?
If thou as yet dost neither love, nor hate,
 Nor choose, nor wish, – resign thyself, be still
 Till I infuse love, hatred, longing, will. –
  I do not deprecate.

A BETTER RESURRECTION

I have no wit, no words, no tears;
　My heart within me like a stone
Is numbed too much for hopes or fears;
　Look right, look left, I dwell alone;
I lift mine eyes, but dimmed with grief
　No everlasting hills I see;
My life is in the falling leaf:
　　O Jesus, quicken me.

My life is like a faded leaf,
　My harvest dwindled to a husk:
Truly my life is void and brief
　And tedious in the barren dusk;
My life is like a frozen thing,
　No bud nor greenness can I see:
Yet rise it shall – the sap of Spring;
　　O Jesus, rise in me.

My life is like a broken bowl,
　A broken bowl that cannot hold
One drop of water for my soul
　Or cordial in the searching cold;
Cast in the fire the perished thing;
　Melt and remould it, till it be
A royal cup for Him, my King:
　　O Jesus, drink of me.

THE THREE ENEMIES

The Flesh

'Sweet, thou art pale.'
        'More pale to see,
Christ hung upon the cruel tree
And bore His Father's wrath for me.'

'Sweet, thou art sad.'
        'Beneath a rod
More heavy, Christ for my sake trod
The winepress of the wrath of God.'

'Sweet, thou art weary.'
        'Not so Christ:
Whose mighty love of me sufficed
For Strength, Salvation, Eucharist.'

'Sweet, thou art footsore.'
        'If I bleed,
His feet have bled; yea, in my need
His Heart once bled for mine indeed.'

The World

'Sweet, thou art young.'
        'So He was young
Who for my sake in silence hung
Upon the Cross with Passion wrung.'

'Look, thou art fair.'
        'He was more fair

Than men, Who deigned for me to wear
A visage marred beyond compare.'

'And thou hast riches.'
        'Daily bread:
All else is His: Who, living, dead,
For me lacked where to lay His Head.'

'And life is sweet.'
        'It was not so
To Him, Whose Cup did overflow
With mine unutterable woe.'

The Devil

'Thou drinkest deep.'
        'When Christ would sup
He drained the dregs from out my cup:
So how should I be lifted up?'

'Thou shalt win Glory.'
        'In the skies,
Lord Jesus, cover up mine eyes
Lest they should look on vanities.'

'Thou shalt have Knowledge.'
        'Helpless dust!
In Thee, O Lord, I put my trust:
Answer Thou for me, Wise and Just.'

'And Might.' –
        'Get thee behind me. Lord,
Who hast redeemed and not abhorred
My soul, oh keep it by Thy Word.'

ONE CERTAINTY

Vanity of vanities, the Preacher saith,
    All things are vanity. The eye and ear
    Cannot be filled with what they see and hear.
Like early dew, or like the sudden breath
Of wind, or like the grass that withereth,
    Is man, tossed to and fro by hope and fear:
    So little joy hath he, so little cheer,
Till all things end in the long dust of death.
To-day is still the same as yesterday,
    To-morrow also even as one of them;
And there is nothing new under the sun:
Until the ancient race of Time be run,
    The old thorns shall grow out of the old stem,
And morning shall be cold and twilight grey.

SWEET DEATH

The sweetest blossoms die.
  And so it was that, going day by day
  Unto the church to praise and pray,
And crossing the green churchyard thoughtfully,
  I saw how on the graves the flowers
  Shed their fresh leaves in showers,
And how their perfume rose up to the sky
  Before it passed away.

The youngest blossoms die.
  They die, and fall and nourish the rich earth
  From which they lately had their birth;
Sweet life, but sweeter death that passeth by
  And is as though it had not been: –
  All colours turn to green;
The bright hues vanish, and the odours fly,
  The grass hath lasting worth.

And youth and beauty die.
  So be it, O my God, Thou God of truth:
  Better than beauty and than youth
Are Saints and Angels, a glad company;
  And Thou, O lord, our Rest and Ease,
  Are better far than these.
Why should we shrink from our full harvest? why
  Prefer to glean with Ruth?

A TESTIMONY

I said of laughter: it is vain.
 Of mirth I said: what profits it?
 Therefore I found a book, and writ
Therein how ease and also pain,
How health and sickness, every one
Is vanity beneath the sun.

Man walks in a vain shadow; he
 Disquieteth himself in vain.
 The things that were shall be again;
The rivers do not fill the sea,
But turn back to their secret source;
The winds too turn upon their course.

Our treasures moth and rust corrupt,
 Or thieves break through and steal, or they
 Make themselves wings and fly away.
One man made merry as he supped,
Nor guessed how when that night grew dim,
His soul would be required of him.

We build our houses on the sand
 Comely withoutside and within;
 But when the winds and rains begin
To beat on them, they cannot stand;
They perish, quickly overthrown,
Loose from the very basement stone.

All things are vanity, I said:
 Yea vanity of vanities.
 The rich man dies; and the poor dies:
The worm feeds sweetly on the dead.

Whate'er thou lackest, keep this trust:
All in the end shall have but dust.

The one inheritance, which best
 And worst alike shall find and share:
 The wicked cease from troubling there,
And there the weary are at rest;
There all the wisdom of the wise
Is vanity of vanities.

Man flourishes as a green leaf,
 And as a leaf doth pass away;
 Or as a shade that cannot stay,
And leaves no track, his course is brief:
Yet doth man hope and fear and plan
Till he is dead: – oh foolish man!

Our eyes cannot be satisfied
 With seeing, nor our ears be filled
 With hearing: yet we plant and build
And buy and make our borders wide;
We gather wealth, we gather care,
But know not who shall be our heir.

Why should we hasten to arise
 So early, and so late take rest?
 Our labour is not good; our best
Hopes fade; our heart is stayed on lies:
Verily, we sow wind; and we
Shall reap the whirlwind, verily.

He who hath little shall not lack;
 He who hath plenty shall decay:
 Our fathers went; we pass away;

Our children follow on our track:
So generations fail, and so
They are renewed, and come and go.

The earth is fattened with our dead;
    She swallows more and doth not cease:
    Therefore her wine and oil increase
And her sheaves are not numberèd;
Therefore her plants are green, and all
Her pleasant trees lusty and tall.

Therefore the maidens cease to sing,
    And the young men are very sad;
    Therefore the sowing is not glad,
And mournful is the harvesting.
Of high and low, of great and small,
Vanity is the lot of all.

A King dwelt in Jerusalem;
    He was the wisest man on earth;
    He had all riches from his birth,
And pleasures till he tired of them;
Then, having tested all things, he
Witnessed that all are vanity.

OLD AND NEW YEAR DITTIES

1.

New Year met me somewhat sad:
  Old Year leaves me tired,
Stripped of favourite things I had,
  Baulked of much desired:
yet farther on my road to-day,
God willing, farther on my way.
New Year coming on apace,
  What have you to give me?
Bring you scathe or bring you grace,
Face me with an honest face,
  You shall not deceive me:
Be it good or ill, be it what you will,
It needs shall help me on my road,
My rugged way to heaven, please God.

2.

Watch with me, men, women, and children dear,
You whom I love, for whom I hope and fear,
Watch with me this last vigil of the year.
Some hug their business, some their pleasure scheme;
Some seize the vacant hour to sleep or dream;
Heart locked in heart some kneel and watch apart.

Watch with me, blessed spirits, who delight
All thro' the holy night to walk in white,
Or take your ease after the long-drawn fight.
I know not if they watch with me: I know
They count this eve of resurrection slow,
And cry 'How long?' with urgent utterance strong.

Watch with me, Jesus, in my loneliness:
Tho' others say me nay, yet say Thou yes;
Tho' others pass me by, stop Thou to bless.
Yea, Thou dost stop with me this vigil night;
To-night of pain, to-morrow of delight:
I, Love, am Thine; Thou, Lord my God, art mine.

3.
Passing away, saith the World, passing away:
Changes, beauty, and youth, sapped day by day:
Thy life never continueth in one stay.
Is the eye waxen dim, is the dark hair changing to grey
That hath won neither laurel nor bay?
I shall clothe myself in Spring and bud in May:
Thou, root-stricken, shalt not rebuild thy decay
On my bosom for aye.
Then I answered: Yea.

Passing away, saith my Soul, passing away:
With its burden of fear and hope, of labour and play,
Hearken what the past doth witness and say:
Rust in thy gold, a moth is in thine array,
A canker is in thy bud, thy leaf must decay.
At midnight, at cockcrow, at morning, one certain day
Lo the Bridegroom shall come and shall not delay;
Watch thou and pray.
Then I answered: Yea.

Passing away, saith my God, passing away:
Winter passeth after the long delay:
New grapes on the vine, new figs on the tender spray,
Turtle calleth turtle in Heaven's May.
Tho' I tarry, wait for Me, trust Me, watch and pray:
Arise, come away, night is past and lo it is day,
My love, My sister, My spouse, thou shalt hear Me say.
Then I answered: Yea.

from THE PRINCE'S PROGRESS

'... Too late for love, too late for joy,
  Too late, too late!
You loitered on the road too long,
  You trifled at the gate:
The enchanted dove upon her branch
  Died without a mate;
The enchanted princess in her tower
  Slept, died, behind the grate;
Her heart was starving all this while
  You made it wait.

'Ten years ago, five years ago,
  One year ago,
Even then you had arrived in time,
  Tho' somewhat slow;
Then you had known her living face
  Which now you cannot know:
The frozen fountain would have leaped,
  The buds gone on to blow,
The warm south wind would have awaked
  To melt the snow.

'Is she fair now as she lies?
  Once she was fair;
Meet queen for any kingly king,
  With gold-dust on her hair.
Now these are poppies in her locks,
  White poppies she must wear;
Must wear a veil to shroud her face
  And the want graven there:
Or is the hunger fed at length,
  Cast off the care?

'We never saw her with a smile
  Or with a frown;
Her bed seemed never soft to her,
  Tho' tossed of down;
She little heeded what she wore,
  Kirtle, or wreath, or gown;
We think her white brows often ached
  Beneath her crown,
Till silvery hairs showed in her locks
  That used to be so brown.

'We never heard her speak in haste;
  Her tones were sweet,
And modulated just so much
  As it was meet:
Her heart sat silent thro' the noise
  And concourse of the street.
There was no hurry in her hands,
  No hurry in her feet;
There was no bliss drew nigh to her,
  That she might run to greet.

‘You should have wept her yesterday,
  Wasting upon her bed:
But wherefore should you weep today
  That she is dead?
Lo, we who love weep not today,
  But crown her royal head.
Let be these poppies that we strew,
  Your roses are too red:
Let be these poppies, not for you
  Cut down and spread.’

SPRING QUIET

Gone were but the Winter,
    Come were but the Spring,
I would go to a covert
    Where the birds sing;

Where in the whitethorn
    Singeth a thrush,
And a robin sings
    In the holly-bush.

Full of fresh scents
    Are the budding boughs
Arching high over
    A cool green house;

Full of sweet scents,
    And whispering air
Which sayeth softly:
    'We spread no snare;

'Here dwell in safety,
    Here dwell alone,
With a clear stream
    And a mossy stone.

'Here the sun shineth
    Most shadily;
Here is heard an echo
    Of the far sea,
    Tho' far off it be.'

A PORTRAIT

I.

She gave up beauty in her tender youth,
  Gave all her hope and joy and pleasant ways;
  She covered up her eyes lest they should gaze
On vanity, and chose the bitter truth.
Harsh towards herself, towards others full of ruth,
  Servant of servants, little known to praise,
  Long prayers and fasts trenched on her nights and days:
She schooled herself to sights and sounds uncouth
That with the poor and stricken she might make
  A home, until the least of all sufficed
Her wants; her own self learned she to forsake,
Counting all earthly gain but hurt and loss.
So with calm will she chose and bore the cross
  And hated all for love of Jesus Christ.

II.

They knelt in silent anguish by her bed,
  And could not weep; but calmly there she lay;
  All pain had left her; and the sun's last ray
Shone through upon her; warming into red
The shady curtains. In her heart she said:
'Heaven opens; I leave these and go away;
  The Bridegroom calls, – shall the Bride seek to stay?'
Then low upon her breast she bowed her head.
O lily flower, O gem of priceless worth,
  O dove with patient voice and patient eyes,
O fruitful vine amid a land of dearth,
  O maid replete with loving purities,
Thou bowedst down thy head with friends on earth
  To raise it with the saints in Paradise.

ONE DAY

I will tell you when they met:
In the limpid days of Spring;
Elder boughs were budding yet,
Oaken boughs looked wintry still,
But primrose and veined violet
In the mossful turf were set,
While meeting birds made haste to sing
And build with right good will.

I will tell you when they parted:
When plenteous Autumn sheaves were brown,
Then they parted heavy-hearted;
The full rejoicing sun looked down
As grand as in the days before;
Only they had lost a crown;
Only to them those days of yore
Could come back nevermore.

When shall they meet? I cannot tell,
Indeed, when they shall meet again,
Except some day in Paradise:
For this they wait, one waits in pain.
Beyond the sea of death love lies
For ever, yesterday, today;
Angels shall ask them, 'Is it well?'
And they shall answer, 'Yea.'

WHAT WOULD I GIVE?

What would I give for a heart of flesh to warm me thro',
Instead of this heart of stone ice-cold whatever I do;
Hard and cold and small, of all hearts the worst of all.

What would I give for words, if only words would come;
But now in its misery my spirit has fallen dumb:
O, merry friends, go your way, I have never a word to say.

What would I give for tears, not smiles but scalding tears,
To wash the black mark clean, and to thaw the frost of years,
To wash the stain ingrain and to make me clean again.

MEMORY

I.

I nursed it in my bosom while it lived,
   I hid it in my heart when it was dead;
In joy I sat alone, even so I grieved
      Alone and nothing said.

I shut the door to face the naked truth,
   I stood alone – I faced the truth alone,
Stripped bare of self-regard or forms or ruth
      Till first and last were shown.

I took the perfect balances and weighed;
   No shaking of my hand disturbed the poise;
Weighed, found it wanting: not a word I said,
      But silent made my choice.

None know the choice I made; I make it still.
   None know the choice I made and broke my heart,
Breaking mine idol: I have braced my will
      Once, chosen for once my part.

I broke it at a blow, I laid it cold,
   Crushed in my deep heart where it used to live.
My heart dies inch by inch; the time grows old,
      Grows old in which I grieve.

II.

I have a room whereinto no one enters
  Save I myself alone:
  There sits a blessed memory on a throne,
There my life centres.

While winter comes and goes – O tedious comer! –
  And while its nip-wind blows;
  While bloom the bloodless lily and warm rose
Of lavish summer.

If any should force entrance he might see there
  One buried yet not dead,
  Before whose face I no more bow my head
Or bend my knee there;

But often in my worn life's autumn weather
  I watch there with clear eyes,
  And think how it will be in Paradise
When we're together.

VANITY OF VANITIES

Ah woe is me for pleasure that is vain,
  Ah woe is me for glory that is past:
  Pleasure that bringeth sorrow at the last,
Glory that at the last bringeth no gain!
So saith the sinking heart; and so again
  It shall say till the mighty angel-blast
  Is blown, making the sun and moon aghast
And showering down the stars like sudden rain.
And evermore men shall go fearfully
  Bending beneath their weight of heaviness;
And ancient men shall lie down wearily,
  And strong men shall rise up in weariness;
Yea, even the young shall answer sighingly,
  Saying one to another: How vain it is!

L.E.L.

'Whose heart was breaking for a little love.'

Downstairs I laugh, I sport and jest with all:
  But in my solitary room above
I turn my face in silence to the wall;
  My heart is breaking for a little love.
    Though winter frosts are done,
    And birds pair every one,
And leaves peep out, for springtide is begun.

I feel no spring, while spring is wellnigh blown,
  I find no nest, while nests are in the grove:
Woe's me for mine own heart that dwells alone,
  My heart that breaketh for a little love.
    While golden in the sun
    Rivulets rise and run,
While lilies bud, for springtide is begun.

All love, are loved, save only I; their hearts
  Beat warm with love and joy, beat full thereof:
They cannot guess, who play the pleasant parts,
  My heart is breaking for a little love.
    While beehives wake and whirr,
    And rabbit thins his fur,
In living spring that sets the world astir.

I deck myself with silks and jewelry,
  I plume myself like any mated dove:
They praise my rustling show, and never see
  My heart is breaking for a little love.
    While sprouts green lavender
    With rosemary and myrrh,
For in quick spring the sap is all astir.

Perhaps some saints in glory guess the truth,
    Perhaps some angels read it as they move,
And cry one to another full of ruth,
    'Her heart is breaking for a little love.'
        Tho' other things have birth,
        And leap and sing for mirth,
When spring-time wakes and clothes and feeds the earth.

Yet saith a saint: 'Take patience for thy scathe';
    Yet saith an angel: 'Wait, for thou shalt prove
True best is last, true life is born of death,
    O thou, heart-broken for a little love!
        Then love shall fill thy girth,
        And love make fat thy dearth,
When new spring builds new heaven and clean new earth.'

EVE

'While I sit at the door,
Sick to gaze within,
Mine eye weepeth sore
For sorrow and sin:
As a tree my sin stands
To darken all lands;
Death is the fruit it bore.

'How have Eden bowers grown
Without Adam to bend them!
How have Eden flowers blown,
Squandering their sweet breath,
Without me to tend them!
The Tree of Life was ours,
Tree twelvefold-fruited,
Most lofty tree that flowers,
Most deeply rooted:
I chose the tree of death.

'Hadst thou but said me nay,
Adam, my brother,
I might have pined away;
I, but none other:
God might have let thee stay
Safe in our garden
By putting me away
Beyond all pardon.

'I, Eve, sad mother
Of all who must live,
I, not another,
Plucked bitterest fruit to give

My friend, husband, lover.
O wanton eyes run over;
Who but I should grieve? –
Cain hath slain his brother:
Of all who must die mother,
Miserable Eve!'

Thus she sat weeping,
Thus Eve, our mother,
Where one lay sleeping
Slain by his brother.
Greatest and least
Each piteous beast
To hear her voice
Forgot his joys
And set aside his feast.

The mouse paused in his walk
And dropped his wheaten stalk;
Grave cattle wagged their heads
In rumination;
The eagle gave a cry
From his cloud station;
Larks on thyme beds
Forbore to mount or sing;
Bees drooped upon the wing;
The raven perched on high
Forgot his ration;
The conies in their rock,
A feeble nation,
Quaked sympathetical;
The mocking-bird left off to mock;
Huge camels knelt as if
In deprecation;

The kind hart's tears were falling;
Chattered the wistful stork;
Dove-voices with a dying fall
Cooed desolation,
Answering grief by grief.

Only the serpent in the dust,
Wriggling and crawling,
Grinned an evil grin and thrust
His tongue out with its fork.

THE QUEEN OF HEARTS

How comes it, Flora, that, whenever we
Play cards together, you invariably,
    However the pack parts,
    Still hold the Queen of Hearts?

I've scanned you with a scrutinising gaze,
Resolved to fathom these your secret ways:
    But, sift them as I will,
    Your ways are secret still.

I cut and shuffle; shuffle, cut, again;
But all my cutting, shuffling, proves in vain:
    Vain hope, vain forethought too;
    The Queen still falls to you.

I dropped her once, prepense; but, ere the deal
Was dealt, your instinct seemed her loss to feel:
    'There should be one card more,'
    You said, and searched the floor.

I cheated once; I made a private notch
In Heart-Queen's back, and kept a lynx-eyed watch;
    Yet such another back
    Deceived me in the pack:

The Queen of Clubs assumed by arts unknown
An imitative dint that seemed my own;
    This notch, not of my doing,
    Misled me to my ruin.

It baffles me to puzzle out the clue,
Which must be skill, or craft, or luck in you:
    Unless, indeed, it be
    Natural affinity.

DOST THOU NOT CARE?

I love and love not: Lord, it breaks my heart
 To love and not to love.
Thou veiled within Thy glory, gone apart
 Into Thy shrine, which is above,
Dost Thou not love me, Lord, or care
 For this mine ill? –
I love thee here or there,
 I will accept thy broken heart, lie still.

Lord, it was well with me in time gone by
 That cometh not again,
When I was fresh and cheerful, who but I?
 I fresh, I cheerful: worn with pain
Now, out of sight and out of heart;
 O Lord, how long? –
I watch thee as thou art,
 I will accept thy fainting heart, be strong.

'Lie still,' 'be strong,' today; but, Lord, tomorrow,
 What of tomorrow, Lord?
Shall there be rest from toil, be truce from sorrow,
 Be living green upon the sward
Now but a barren grave to me,
 Be joy for sorrow? –
Did I not die for thee?
 Did I not live for thee? Leave Me tomorrow.

WEARY IN WELL-DOING

I would have gone; God bade me stay:
   I would have worked; God bade me rest.
He broke my will from day to day,
   He read my yearnings unexpressed
      And said them nay.

Now I would stay; God bids me go:
   Now I would rest; God bids me work.
He breaks my heart tossed to and fro,
   My soul is wrung with doubts that lurk
      And vex it so.

I go, Lord, where Thou sendest me;
   Day after day I plod and moil:
But, Christ my God, when will it be
   That I may let alone my toil
      And rest with Thee?

GOOD FRIDAY

Am I a stone, and not a sheep,
  That I can stand, O Christ, beneath Thy cross,
  To number drop by drop Thy blood's slow loss,
And yet not weep?

Not so those women loved
  Who with exceeding grief lamented Thee;
  Not so fallen Peter, weeping bitterly;
Not so the thief was moved;

Not so the Sun and Moon
  Which hid their faces in a starless sky,
A horror of great darkness at broad noon –
  I, only I.

Yet give not o'er,
  But seek Thy sheep, true Shepherd of the flock;
Greater than Moses, turn and look once more
  And smite a rock.

THE LOWEST PLACE

Give me the lowest place: not that I dare
  Ask for that lowest place, but Thou hast died
That I might live and share
  Thy glory by Thy side.

Give me the lowest place: or if for me
  That lowest place too high, make one more low
Where I may sit and see
  My God and love Thee so.

Poems Added in Goblin Market, The Prince's Progress and Other Poems (1875)

A DIRGE

Why were you born when the snow was falling?
You should have come to the cuckoo's calling,
Or when grapes are green in the cluster,
Or, at least, when lithe swallows muster
For their far off flying
From summer dying.

Why did you die when the lambs were cropping?
You should have died at the apples' dropping,
When the grasshopper comes to trouble,
And the wheat-fields are sodden stubble,
And all winds go sighing
For sweet things dying.

DEAD HOPE

Hope new born one pleasant morn
 Died at even;
Hope dead lives nevermore.
 No, not in heaven.

If his shroud were but a cloud
 To weep itself away;
Or were he buried underground
 To sprout some day!
But dead and gone is dead and gone
 Vainly wept upon.

Nought we place above his face
 To mark the spot,
But it shows a barren place
 In our lot.
Hope has birth no more on earth
 Morn or even;
Hope dead lives nevermore,
 No, not in heaven.

A DAUGHTER OF EVE

A fool I was to sleep at noon,
  And wake when night is chilly
Beneath the comfortless cold moon;
A fool to pluck my rose too soon,
  A fool to snap my lily.

My garden-plot I have not kept;
  Faded and all-forsaken,
I weep as I have never wept:
Oh it was summer when I slept,
  It's winter now I waken.

Talk what you please of future Spring
  And sun-warmed sweet tomorrow: –
Stripped bare of hope and everything,
No more to laugh, no more to sing,
  I sit alone with sorrow.

AMOR MUNDI

'Oh, where are you going with your love-locks flowing
  On the west wind blowing along this valley track?'
'The downhill path is easy, come with me an it please ye,
  We shall escape the uphill by never turning back.'

So they two went together in glowing August weather,
  The honey-breathing heather lay to their left and right;
And dear she was to doat on, her swift feet seemed to float on
  The air like soft twin pigeons too sportive to alight.

'Oh, what is that in heaven where grey cloud-flakes are seven,
  Where blackest clouds hang riven just at the rainy skirt?'
'Oh, that's a meteor sent us, a message dumb, portentous, –
  An undeciphered solemn signal of help or hurt.'

'Oh, what is that glides quickly where velvet flowers grow thickly,
  Their scent comes rich and sickly?' – 'A scaled and hooded worm.'
'Oh, what's that in the hollow, so pale I quake to follow?'
  'Oh, that's a thin dead body which waits the eternal term.'

'Turn again, O my sweetest, – turn again, false and fleetest:
  This beaten way whereof thou beatest I fear is hell's own track.'
'Nay, too steep for hill-mounting;nay, too late for cost-counting:
  This downhill path is easy, but there's no turning back.'

A CHRISTMAS CAROL

In the bleak midwinter,
   Frosty wind made moan,
Earth stood hard as iron
   Water like a stone;
Snow had fallen, snow on snow,
   Snow on snow,
In the bleak midwinter,
   Long ago.

Our God, Heaven cannot hold Him,
   Nor earth sustain;
Heaven and earth shall flee away
   When He comes to reign:
In the bleak mid-winter
   A stable-place sufficed
The Lord God Almighty
   Jesus Christ.

Enough for Him whom cherubim
   Worship night and day,
A breastful of milk
   And a mangerful of hay;
Enough for Him whom angels
   Fall down before,
The ox and ass and camel
   Which adore.

Angels and archangels
   May have gathered there,
Cherubim and seraphim
   Thronged the air,
But only His mother
   In her maiden bliss
Worshipped the Beloved
   With a kiss.

What can I give Him,
   Poor as I am?
If I were a shepherd
   I would bring a lamb,
If I were a wise man
   I would do my part, –
Yet what I can I give Him,
   Give my heart.

WHEN MY HEART IS VEXED, I WILL COMPLAIN

'O Lord, how canst Thou say Thou lovest me?
  Me whom Thou settest in a barren land,
  Hungry and thirsty on the burning sand,
Hungry and thirsty where no waters be
Nor shadows of date-bearing tree: –
O Lord, how canst Thou say Thou lovest me?'

'I came from Edom by as parched a track,
  As rough a track beneath My bleeding feet.
  I came from Edom seeking thee, and sweet
I counted bitterness; I turned not back
But counted life as death, and trod
The winepress all alone: and I am God.'

'Yet, Lord, how canst Thou say Thou lovest me?
  For Thou art strong to comfort: and could I
  But comfort one I love, who, like to die,
Lifts feeble hands and eyes that fail to see
In one last prayer for comfort – nay,
I could not stand aside or turn away.'

'Alas! thou knowest that for thee I died
  For thee I thirsted with the dying thirst;
  I, Blessed, for thy sake was counted cursed,
In sight of men and angels crucified:
All this and more I bore to prove
My love, and wilt thou yet mistrust My love?'

‘Lord, I am fain to think Thou lovest me,
  For Thou art all in all and I am Thine;
  And lo! Thy love is better than new wine,
And I am sick of love in loving Thee.
But dost Thou love me? speak and save,
For jealousy is cruel as the grave.’

‘Nay, if thy love is not an empty breath
  My love is as thine own – deep answers deep.
  Peace, peace: I give to My beloved sleep,
Not death but sleep, for love is strong as death:
Take patience; sweet thy sleep shall be,
Yea, thou shalt wake in Paradise with Me.’

'IN THE MEADOW – WHAT IN THE MEADOW?'

In the meadow – what in the meadow?
Bluebells, buttercups, meadowsweet,
And fairy rings for the children's feet
　　　In the meadow.

In the garden – what in the garden?
Jacob's-ladder and Solomon's-seal,
And Love lies-bleeding beside All-heal
　　　In the garden.

'CRYING, MY LITTLE ONE, FOOTSORE AND WEARY'

Crying, my little one, footsore and weary?
 Fall asleep, pretty one, warm on my shoulder:
I must tramp on through the winter night dreary,
 While the snow falls on me colder and colder.

You are my one, and I have not another;
 Sleep soft, my darling, my trouble and treasure;
Sleep warm and soft in the arms of your mother,
 Dreaming of pretty things, dreaming of pleasure.

‘MARGARET HAS A MILKING-PAIL’

Margaret has a milking-pail,
   And she rises early;
Thomas has a threshing-flail,
   And he’s up betimes.

Sometimes crossing through the grass
   Where the dew lies pearly,
They say ‘Good morrow’ as they pass
   By the leafy limes.

'JANUARY COLD DESOLATE'

January cold desolate;
February all dripping wet;
March wind ranges;
April changes;
Birds sing in tune
  To flowers of May,
And sunny June
  Brings longest day;
In scorched July
The storm-clouds fly
Lightning torn;
August bears corn,
September fruit;
In rough October
Earth must disrobe her;
Stars fall and shoot
In keen November;
And night is long
And cold is strong
In bleak December.

‘WHO HAS SEEN THE WIND?’

Who has seen the wind?
    Neither I nor you:
But when the leaves hang trembling,
    The wind is passing through.

Who has seen the wind?
    Neither you nor I:
But when the trees bow down their heads,
    The wind is passing by.

THE KEY-NOTE

Where are the songs I used to know,
  Where are the notes I used to sing?
  I have forgotten everything
I used to know so long ago;
Summer has followed after Spring;
  Now Autumn is so shrunk and sere,
I scarcely think a sadder thing
  Can be the Winter of my year.

Yet Robin sings thro' Winter's rest,
  When bushes put their berries on;
  While they their ruddy jewels don,
He sings out of a ruddy breast;
The hips and haws and ruddy breast
  Make one spot warm where snowflakes lie,
They break and cheer the unlovely rest
  Of Winter's pause – and why not I?

PASTIME

A boat amid the ripples, drifting, rocking,
 Two idle people, without pause or aim;
While in the ominous west there gathers darkness
  Flushed with flame.

A haycock in a hayfield backing, lapping,
 Two drowsy people pillowed round about;
While in the ominous west across the darkness
  Flame leaps out.

Better a wrecked life than a life so aimless,
 Better a wrecked life than a life so soft;
The ominous west glooms thundering, with its fire
  Lit aloft.

ITALIA, IO TI SALUTO!

To come back from the sweet South, to the North
  Where I was born, bred, look to die;
Come back to do my day's work in its day,
    Play out my play –
  Amen, amen, say I.

To see no more the country half my own,
  Nor hear the half familiar speech,
Amen, I say; I turn to that bleak North
    Whence I came forth –
  The South lies out of reach.

But when our swallows fly back to the South,
  To the sweet South, to the sweet South,
The tears may come again into my eyes
    On the old wise,
  And the sweet name to my mouth.

YET A LITTLE WHILE

I dreamed and did not seek: today I seek
Who can no longer dream;
But now am all behindhand, waxen weak,
And dazed amid so many things that gleam
Yet are not what they seem.

I dreamed and did not work: today I work
Kept wide awake by care
And loss, and perils dimly guessed to lurk;
I work and reap not, while my life goes bare
And void in wintry air.

I hope indeed; but hope itself is fear
Viewed on the sunny side;
I hope, and disregard the world that's here,
The prizes drawn, the sweet things that betide;
I hope, and I abide.

MONNA INNOMINATA

A Sonnet Of Sonnets

Beatrice, immortalised by 'altissimo poeta ... cotanto amante;' Laura, celebrated by a great though an inferior bard, – have alike paid the exceptional penalty of exceptional honor, and have come down to us resplendent with charms, but (at least, to my apprehension) scant of attractiveness.

These heroines of world-wide fame were preceded by a bevy of unnamed ladies 'donne innominate' sung by a school of less conspicuous poets; and in that land and that period which gave simultaneous birth to Catholics, to Albigenses, and to Troubadours, one can imagine many a lady as sharing her lover's poetic aptitude, while the barrier between them might be one held sacred by both, yet not such as to render mutual love incompatible with mutual honour.

Had such a lady spoken for herself, the portrait left us might have appeared more tender, if less dignified, than any drawn even by a devoted friend. Or had the Great Poetess of our own day and nation only been unhappy instead of happy, her circumstances would have invited her to bequeath to us, in lieu of the 'Portuguese Sonnets,' an inimitable 'donna innominata' drawn not from fancy but from feeling, and worthy to occupy a niche beside Beatrice and Laura.

'Lo di che han detto a' dolci amici addio.' – Dante.
'Amor, con quanto sforzo oggi mi vinci!' – Petrarca.

Come back to me, who wait and watch for you: –
    Or come not yet, for it is over then,
    And long it is before you come again,
So far between my pleasures are and few.
While, when you come not, what I do I do
    Thinking 'Now when he comes,' my sweetest 'when:'
    For one man is my world of all the men
This wide world holds; O love, my world is you.
Howbeit, to meet you grows almost a pang
    Because the pang of parting comes so soon;
    My hope hangs waning, waxing, like a moon
        Between the heavenly days on which we meet:
Ah me, but where are now the songs I sang
        When life was sweet because you called them sweet?

2.

'Era già l'ora che volge il desio.' – Dante.
'Ricorro al tempo ch' io vi vidi prima.' – Petrarca.

I wish I could remember that first day,
    First hour, first moment of your meeting me,
    If bright or dim the season, it might be
Summer or Winter for aught I can say;
So unrecorded did it slip away,
    So blind was I to see and to foresee,
    So dull to mark the budding of my tree
That would not blossom yet for many a May.
If only I could recollect it, such
    A day of days! I let it come and go
    As traceless as a thaw of bygone snow;
It seemed to mean so little, meant so much;

If only now I could recall that touch,
    First touch of hand in hand – Did one but know!

3.

'O ombre vane, fuor che ne l'aspetto!' – Dante.
'Immaginata guida la conduce.' – Petrarca.

I dream of you to wake: would that I might
    Dream of you and not wake but slumber on;
    Nor find with dreams the dear companion gone,
As Summer ended Summer birds take flight.
In happy dreams I hold you full in sight,
    I blush again who waking look so wan;
    Brighter than sunniest day that ever shone,
In happy dreams your smile makes day of night.
Thus only in a dream we are at one,
    Thus only in a dream we give and take
        The faith that maketh rich who take or give;
    If thus to sleep is sweeter than to wake,
        To die were surely sweeter than to live,
Though there be nothing new beneath the sun.

4.

'Poca favilla gran fiamma seconda.' – Dante.
'Ogni altra cosa, ogni pensier va fore,
E sol ivi con voi rimansi amore.' – Petrarca.

I loved you first: but afterwards your love
    Outsoaring mine, sang such a loftier song
As drowned the friendly cooings of my dove.
    Which owes the other most? my love was long,
    And yours one moment seemed to wax more strong;
I loved and guessed at you, you construed me
And loved me for what might or might not be –

Nay, weights and measures do us both a wrong.
For verily love knows not 'mine' or 'thine;'
With separate 'I' and 'thou' free love has done,
For one is both and both are one in love:
Rich love knows nought of 'thine that is not mine;'
Both have the strength and both the length thereof,
Both of us of the love which makes us one.

5.

'Amor che a nulla amato amar perdona.' – Dante.
'Amor m'addusse in si gioiosa spene.' – Petrarca.

O my heart's heart, and you who are to me
More than myself myself, God be with you,
Keep you in strong obedience leal and true
To Him whose noble service setteth free,
Give you all good we see or can foresee,
Make your joys many and your sorrows few,
Bless you in what you bear and what you do,
Yea, perfect you as He would have you be.
So much for you; but what for me, dear friend?
To love you without stint and all I can
To-day, to-morrow, world without an end;
To love you much and yet to love you more,
As Jordan at his flood sweeps either shore;
Since woman is the helpmeet made for man.

6.

'Or puoi la quantitate
Comprender de l'amor che a te mi scalda.' – Dante.
'Non vo' che da tal nodo amor mi scioglia.' – Petrarca.

Trust me, I have not earned your dear rebuke,
I love, as you would have me, God the most;

Would lose not Him, but you, must one be lost,
Nor with Lot's wife cast back a faithless look
Unready to forego what I forsook;
This say I, having counted up the cost,
This, though I be the feeblest of God's host,
The sorriest sheep Christ shepherds with His crook,
Yet while I love my God the most, I deem
That I can never love you overmuch;
I love Him more, so let me love you too;
Yea, as I apprehend it, love is such
I cannot love you if I love not Him,
I cannot love Him if I love not you.

7.

'Qui primavera sempre ed ogni frutto.' – Dante.
'Ragionando con meco ed io con lui.' – Petrarca.

'Love me, for I love you' – and answer me,
'Love me, for I love you' – so shall we stand
As happy equals in the flowering land
Of love, that knows not a dividing sea.
Love builds the house on rock and not on sand,
Love laughs what while the winds rave desperately;
And who hath found love's citadel unmanned?
And who hath held in bonds love's liberty?
My heart's a coward though my words are brave –
We meet so seldom, yet we surely part
So often; there's a problem for your art!
Still I find comfort in his Book, who saith,
Though jealousy be cruel as the grave,
And death be strong, yet love is strong as death.

8.

'Come dicesse a Dio: D'altro non calme.' – Dante.
'Spero trovar pietà non che perdono.' – Petrarca.

'I, if I perish, perish' – Esther spake:
And bride of life or death she made her fair
In all the lustre of her perfumed hair
And smiles that kindle longing but to slake.
She put on pomp of loveliness, to take
Her husband through his eyes at unaware;
She spread abroad her beauty for a snare,
Harmless as doves and subtle as a snake.
She trapped him with one mesh of silken hair,
She vanquished him by wisdom of her wit,
And built her people's house that it should stand: –
If I might take my life so in my hand,
And for my love to Love put up my prayer,
And for love's sake by Love be granted it!

9.

'O dignitosa coscienza e netta!' – Dante.
'Spirto più acceso di virtuti ardenti.' – Petrarca.

Thinking of you, and all that was, and all
That might have been and now can never be,
I feel your honored excellence, and see
Myself unworthy of the happier call:
For woe is me who walk so apt to fall,
So apt to shrink afraid, so apt to flee,
Apt to lie down and die (ah, woe is me!)
Faithless and hopeless turning to the wall.
And yet not hopeless quite nor faithless quite,
Because not loveless; love may toil all night,
But take at morning; wrestle till the break

Of day, but then wield power with God and man: –
So take I heart of grace as best I can,
Ready to spend and be spent for your sake.

10.

'Con miglior corso e con migliore stella.' – Dante.
'La vita fugge e non s'arresta un' ora.' – Petrarca.

Time flies, hope flags, life plies a wearied wing;
Death following hard on life gains ground apace;
Faith runs with each and rears an eager face,
Outruns the rest, makes light of everything,
Spurns earth, and still finds breath to pray and sing;
While love ahead of all uplifts his praise,
Still asks for grace and still gives thanks for grace,
Content with all day brings and night will bring.
Life wanes; and when love folds his wings above
Tired hope, and less we feel his conscious pulse,
Let us go fall asleep, dear friend, in peace:
A little while, and age and sorrow cease;
A little while, and life reborn annuls
Loss and decay and death, and all is love.

11.

'Vien dietro a me e lascia dir le genti.' – Dante.
'Contando i casi della vita nostra.' – Petrarca.

Many in aftertimes will say of you
'He loved her' – while of me what will they say?
Not that I loved you more than just in play,
For fashion's sake as idle women do.
Even let them prate; who know not what we knew
Of love and parting in exceeding pain,
Of parting hopeless here to meet again,

Hopeless on earth, and heaven is out of view.
But by my heart of love laid bare to you,
My love that you can make not void nor vain,
Love that foregoes you but to claim anew
Beyond this passage of the gate of death,
I charge you at the Judgment make it plain
My love of you was life and not a breath.

12.

'Amor, che ne la mente mi ragiona.' – Dante.
'Amor vien nel bel viso di costei.' – Petrarca.

If there be any one can take my place
And make you happy whom I grieve to grieve,
Think not that I can grudge it, but believe
I do commend you to that nobler grace,
That readier wit than mine, that sweeter face;
Yea, since your riches make me rich, conceive
I too am crowned, while bridal crowns I weave,
And thread the bridal dance with jocund pace.
For if I did not love you, it might be
That I should grudge you some one dear delight;
But since the heart is yours that was mine own,
Your pleasure is my pleasure, right my right,
Your honorable freedom makes me free,
And you companioned I am not alone.

13.

'E drizzeremo gli occhi al Primo Amore.' – Dante.
'Ma trovo peso non da le mie braccia.' – Petrarca.

If I could trust mine own self with your fate,
Shall I not rather trust it in God's hand?
Without Whose Will one lily doth not stand,

Nor sparrow fall at his appointed date;
Who numbereth the innumerable sand,
Who weighs the wind and water with a weight,
To Whom the world is neither small nor great,
Whose knowledge foreknew every plan we planned.
Searching my heart for all that touches you,
I find there only love and love's goodwill
Helpless to help and impotent to do,
Of understanding dull, of sight most dim;
And therefore I commend you back to Him
Whose love your love's capacity can fill.

14.

'E la Sua Volontade è nostra pace.' – Dante.
'Sol con questi pensier, con altre chiome.' – Petrarca.

Youth gone, and beauty gone if ever there
Dwelt beauty in so poor a face as this;
Youth gone and beauty, what remains of bliss?
I will not bind fresh roses in my hair,
To shame a cheek at best but little fair, –
Leave youth his roses, who can bear a thorn, –
I will not seek for blossoms anywhere,
Except such common flowers as blow with corn.
Youth gone and beauty gone, what doth remain?
The longing of a heart pent up forlorn,
A silent heart whose silence loves and longs;
The silence of a heart which sang its songs
While youth and beauty made a summer morn,
Silence of love that cannot sing again.

DE PROFUNDIS

Oh why is heaven built so far,
  Oh why is earth set so remote?
I cannot reach the nearest star
    That hangs afloat.

I would not care to reach the moon,
  One round monotonous of change;
Yet even she repeats her tune
    Beyond my range.

I never watch the scattered fire
  Of stars, or sun's far-trailing train,
But all my heart is one desire,
    And all in vain:

For I am bound with fleshly bands,
  Joy, beauty, lie beyond my scope;
I strain my heart, I stretch my hands,
    And catch at hope.

A LIFE'S PARALLELS

Never on this side of the grave again,
  On this side of the river,
On this side of the garner of the grain,
          Never, –

Ever while time flows on and on and on,
  That narrow noiseless river,
Ever while corn bows heavy-headed, wan,
          Ever, –

Never despairing, often fainting, rueing,
  But looking back, ah never!
Faint yet pursuing, faint yet still pursuing
          Ever.

GOLDEN SILENCES

There is silence that saith, 'Ah me!'
  There is silence that nothing saith;
    One the silence of life forlorn,
  One the silence of death;
One is, and the other shall be.

One we know and have known for long,
  One we know not, but we shall know,
    All we who have ever been born;
  Even so, be it so, –
There is silence, despite a song.

Sowing day is a silent day,
  Resting night is a silent night;
    But whoso reaps the ripened corn
  Shall shout in his delight,
While silences vanish away.

MARIANA

Not for me marring or making,
Not for me giving or taking;
  I love my Love and he loves not me,
I love my Love and my heart is breaking.

Sweet is Spring in its lovely showing,
Sweet the violet veiled in blowing,
  Sweet it is to love and be loved;
Ah, sweet knowledge beyond my knowing!

Who sighs for love sighs but for pleasure,
Who wastes for love hoards up a treasure;
  Sweet to be loved and take no count,
Sweet it is to love without measure.

Sweet my Love whom I loved to try for,
Sweet my Love whom I love and sigh for,
  Will you once love me and sigh for me,
You my Love whom I love and die for?

ONE SEA-SIDE GRAVE

Unmindful of the roses,
  Unmindful of the thorn,
A reaper tired reposes
  Among his gathered corn:
  So might I, till the morn!

Cold as the cold Decembers,
  Past as the days that set,
While only one remembers
  And all the rest forget, –
  But one remembers yet.

A HOPE CAROL

A night was near, a day was near,
  Between a day and night
I heard sweet voices calling clear,
    Calling me:
I heard a whirr of wing on wing,
  But could not see the sight;
I long to see my birds that sing,
    I long to see.

Below the stars, beyond the moon,
  Between the night and day,
I heard a rising falling tune
    Calling me:
I long to see the pipes and strings
  Whereon such minstrels play;
I long to see each face that sings, –
    I long to see.

Today or may be not today,
  Tonight or not tonight;
All voices that command or pray,
    Calling me,
Shall kindle in my soul such fire,
  And in my eyes such light,
That I shall see that heart's desire
    I long to see.

A CANDLEMAS DIALOGUE

'Love brought Me down: and cannot love make thee
Carol for joy to Me?
Hear cheerful robin carol from his tree,
Who owes not half to Me
I won for thee.'

'Yea, Lord, I hear his carol's wordless voice;
And well may he rejoice
Who hath not heard of death's discordant noise.
So might I too rejoice
With such a voice.'

'True, thou hast compassed death: but hast not thou
The tree of life's own bough?
Am I not Life and Resurrection now?
My Cross, balm-bearing bough
For such as thou.'

'Ah me, Thy Cross! – but that seems far away;
Thy Cradle-song today
I too would raise and worship Thee and pray:
Not empty, Lord, today
Send me away.'

'If thou wilt not go empty, spend thy store;
And I will give thee more,
Yea, make thee ten times richer than before.
Give more and give yet more
Out of thy store.'

‘Because Thou givest me Thyself, I will
Thy blessed word fulfil,
Give with both hands, and hoard by giving still:
Thy pleasure to fulfil,
And work Thy Will.’

HE CANNOT DENY HIMSELF

Love still is Love, and doeth all things well,
Whether He shows me heaven or hell
    Or earth in her decay
    Passing away
    On a day.

Love still is Love, tho' He should say, 'Depart.'
And break my incorrigible heart,
    And set me out of sight
    Widowed of light
    In the night.

Love still is Love, is Love, if He should say,
'Come,' on that uttermost dread day;
    'Come,' unto very me,
    'Come where I be,
    Come and see.'

Love still is Love, whatever comes to pass:
O Only Love, make me Thy glass,
    Thy pleasure to fulfil
    By loving still
    Come what will.

BALM IN GILEAD

Heartsease I found, where Love-lies-bleeding
  Empurpled all the ground:
Whatever flowers I missed unheeding,
  Heartsease I found.

  Yet still my garden mound
Stood sore in need of watering, weeding,
  And binding growths unbound.

Ah, when shades fell to light succeeding
  I scarcely dared look round:
'Love-lies-bleeding' was all my pleading,
  Heartsease I found.

ADVENT SUNDAY

Behold, the Bridegroom cometh: go ye out
With lighted lamps and garlands round about
To meet Him in a rapture with a shout.

It may be at the midnight, black as pitch,
Earth shall cast up her poor, cast up her rich.

It may be at the crowing of the cock
Earth shall upheave her depth, uproot her rock.

For lo, the Bridegroom fetcheth home the Bride:
His Hands are Hands she knows, she knows His Side.

Like pure Rebekah at the appointed place,
Veiled, she unveils her face to meet His Face.

Like great Queen Esther in her triumphing,
She triumphs in the Presence of her King.

His Eyes are as a Dove's, and she's Dove-eyed;
He knows His lovely mirror, sister, Bride.

He speaks with Dove-voice of exceeding love,
And she with love-voice of an answering Dove.

Behold, the Bridegroom cometh: go we out
With lamps ablaze and garlands round about
To meet Him in a rapture with a shout.

ADVENT

Sooner or later: yet at last
The Jordan must be past;

It may be he will overflow
His banks the day we go;

It may be that his cloven deep
Will stand up on a heap.

Sooner or later: yet one day
We all must pass that way;

Each man, each woman, humbled, pale,
Pass veiled within the veil;

Child, parent, bride, companion,
Alone, alone, alone.

For none a ransom can be paid,
A suretyship be made:

I, bent by mine own burden, must
Enter my house of dust;

I, rated to the full amount,
Must render mine account.

When earth and sea shall empty all
Their graves of great and small;

When earth wrapped in a fiery flood
Shall no more hide her blood;

When mysteries shall be revealed;
All secrets be unsealed;

When things of night, when things of shame,
Shall find at last a name,

Pealed for a hissing and a curse
Throughout the universe:

Then, Awful Judge, most Awful God,
Then cause to bud Thy rod,

To bloom with blossoms, and to give
Almonds; yea, bid us live.

I please Thyself with Thee, I plead
Thee in our utter need:

Jesus, most Merciful of Men,
Show mercy on us then;

Lord God of Mercy and of men,
Show mercy on us then.

CHRISTMASTIDE

Love came down at Christmas,
  Love all lovely, love divine;
Love was born at Christmas,
  Star and angels gave the sign.

Worship we the Godhead,
  Love incarnate, love divine;
Worship we our Jesus:
  But wherewith for sacred sign?

Love shall be our token,
  Love shall be yours and love be mine,
Love to God and to all men,
  Love for plea and gift and sign.

ST JOHN THE APOSTLE

Earth cannot bar flame from ascending,
Hell cannot bind light from descending,
Death cannot finish life never ending.

Eagle and sun gaze at each other,
Eagle at sun, brother at Brother,
Loving in peace and joy one another.

O St. John, with chains for thy wages,
Strong thy rock where the storm-blast rages,
Rock of refuge, the Rock of Ages.

Rome hath passed with her awful voice,
Earth is passing with all her joys,
Heaven shall pass away with a noise.

So from us all follies that please us,
So from us all falsehoods that ease us,–
Only all saints abide with their Jesus.

Jesus, in love looking down hither,
Jesus, by love draw us up thither,
That we in Thee may abide together.

EPIPHANY

'Lord Babe, if Thou art He
We sought for patiently,
Where is Thy court?
Hither may prophecy and star resort;
Men heed not their report.' –
  'Bow down and worship, righteous man:
  This Infant of a span
  Is He man sought for since the world began!' –
'Then, Lord, accept my gold, too base a thing
For Thee, of all kings King.' –

'Lord Babe, despite Thy youth
I hold Thee of a truth
Both Good and Great:
But wherefore dost Thou keep so mean a state,
Low-lying desolate?' –
  'Bow down and worship, righteous seer:
  The Lord our God is here
  Approachable, Who bids us all draw near.' –
'Wherefore to Thee I offer frankincense,
Thou Sole Omnipotence.' –

'But I have only brought
Myrrh; no wise afterthought
Instructed me
To gather pearls or gems, or choice to see
Coral or ivory.' –
  'Not least thine offering proves thee wise:
  For myrrh means sacrifice,
  And He that lives, this Same is He that dies.' –
'Then here is myrrh: alas! yea woe is me
That myrrh befitteth Thee.' –

Myrrh, frankincense, and gold:
And lo from wintry fold
Good-will doth bring
A Lamb, the innocent likeness of this King
Whom stars and seraphs sing:
   And lo! the bird of love, a Dove,
   Flutters and coos above:
   And Dove and Lamb and Babe agree in love: –
Come all mankind, come all creation hither,
Come, worship Christ together.

EPIPHANYTIDE

Trembling before Thee we fall down to adore Thee,
Shamefaced and trembling we lift our eyes to Thee:
O First and with the last! annul our ruined past,
Rebuild us to Thy glory, set us free
From sin and from sorrow to fall down and worship
Thee.

Full of pity view us, stretch Thy sceptre to us,
Bid us live that we may give ourselves to Thee:
O faithful Lord and True! stand up for us and do,
Make us lovely, make us new, set us free –
Heart and soul and spirit – to bring all and worship
Thee.

VIGIL OF THE PRESENTATION

Long and dark the nights, dim and short the days,
Mounting weary heights on our weary ways,
  Thee our God we praise.
Scaling heavenly heights by unearthly ways,
Thee our God we praise all our nights and days,
  Thee our God we praise.

FEAST OF THE PRESENTATION

O Firstfruits of our grain,
Infant and Lamb appointed to be slain,
A Virgin and two doves were all Thy train,
With one old man for state,
When Thou didst enter first Thy Father's gate.

Since then Thy train hath been
Freeman and bondman, bishop, king and queen,
With flaming candles and with garlands green:
Oh happy all who wait
One day or thousand days around Thy gate!

And these have offered Thee,
Beside their hearts, great stores for charity,
Gold, frankincense, and myrrh; if such may be
For savour or for state
Within the threshold of Thy golden gate.

Then snowdrops and my heart
I'll bring, to find those blacker than Thou art:
Yet, loving Lord, accept us in good part;
And give me grace to wait,
A bruised reed bowed low before Thy gate.

THE PURIFICATION OF ST MARY THE VIRGIN

Purity born of a Maid:
Was such a Virgin defiled?
Nay, by no shade of a shade.
She offered her gift of pure love,
A dove with a fair fellow-dove,
A dove with a fair fellow-dove.
She offered her Innocent Child
The Essence and Author of Love;
The Lamb that indwelt by the Dove
Was spotless and holy and mild;
More pure than all other,
More pure than His Mother,
Her God and Redeemer and Child.

VIGIL OF THE ANNUNCIATION

All weareth, all wasteth,
All flitteth, all hasteth,
All of flesh and time: –
Sound, sweet heavenly chime,
Ring in the unutterable eternal prime.

Man hopeth, man feareth,
Man droopeth: – Christ cheereth,
Compassing release,
Comforting with peace,
Promising rest where strife and anguish cease.

Saints waking, saints sleeping,
Rest well in safe keeping;
Well they rest today
While they watch and pray,
But their tomorrow's rest what tongue shall say?

VIGIL OF ST PETER

O Jesu, gone so far apart
  Only my heart can follow Thee,
That look which pierced St Peter's heart
    Turn now on me.

Thou Who dost search me thro' and thro'
  And mark the crooked ways I went,
Look on me, Lord, and make me too
    Thy penitent.

ST PETER

'Launch out into the deep,' Christ spake of old
  To Peter: and he launched into the deep;
  Strengthened should tempest wake which lay asleep,
Strengthened to suffer heat or suffer cold.
Thus, in Christ's Prescience: patient to behold
  A fall, a rise, a scaling Heaven's high steep;
  Prescience of Love, which deigned to overleap
The mire of human errors manifold.
Lord, Lover of Thy Peter, and of him
  Beloved with craving of a humbled heart
    Which eighteen hundred years have satisfied;
Hath he his throne among Thy Seraphim
  Who love? or sits he on a throne apart,
    Unique, near Thee, to love Thee human-eyed?

St Peter once: 'Lord, doest Thou wash my feet?' –
  Much more I say: Lord, dost Thou stand and knock
  At my closed heart more rugged than a rock,
Bolted and barred, for Thy soft touch unmet,
Nor garnished in any wise made sweet?
  Owls roost within and dancing satyrs mock.
  Lord, I have heard the crowing of the cock
And have not wept: ah, Lord, thou knowest it.
Yet still I hear Thee knocking, still I hear:
  'Open to Me, look on Me eye to eye,
    That I may wring thy heart and make it whole;
And teach thee love because I hold thee dear
    And sup with thee in gladness soul with soul,
  And sup with thee in glory by and by.'

SUNDAY BEFORE ADVENT

The end of all things is at hand. We all
   Stand in the balance trembling as we stand;
Or if not trembling, tottering to a fall.
   The end of all things is at hand.

   O hearts of men, covet the unending land!
   O hearts of men, covet the musical,
   Sweet, never-ending waters of that strand!

While Earth shows poor, a slippery rolling ball,
   And Hell looms vast, a gulf unplumbed, unspanned,
And Heaven flings wide its gates to great and small,
   The end of all things is at hand.

LAY UP FOR YOURSELVES TREASURES IN HEAVEN

Treasure plies a feather,
  Pleasure spreadeth wings,
Taking flight together, –
  Ah! my cherished things.

Fly away, poor pleasure,
  That art so brief a thing:
Fly away, poor treasure,
  That hast so swift a wing.

Pleasure, to be pleasure,
  Must come without a wing;
Treasure, to be treasure,
  Must be a stable thing.

Treasure without feather,
  Pleasure without wings,
Elsewhere dwell together
  And are heavenly things.

SAPPHO

I sigh at day-dawn, and I sigh
When the dull day is passing by.
I sigh at evening, and again
I sigh when night brings sleep to men.
Oh! it were better far to die
Than thus for ever mourn and sigh,
And in death's dreamless sleep to be
Unconscious that none weep for me;
Eased from my weight of heaviness,
Forgetful of forgetfulness,
Resting from pain and care and sorrow
Through the long night that knows no morrow;
Living unloved, to die unknown,
Unwept, untended and alone.

TWO THOUGHTS OF DEATH

1.

Her heart that loved me once is rottenness
  Now and corruption; and her life is dead
  That was to have been one with mine she said.
The earth must lie with such a cruel stress
On her eyes where the white lids used to press;
  Foul worms fill up her mouth so sweet and red;
  Foul worms are underneath her graceful head.
Yet these, being born of her from nothingness
These worms are certainly flesh of her flesh. –
  How is it that the grass is rank and green,
And the dew dropping rose is brave and fresh
Above what was so sweeter far than they?
Even as her beauty hath passed quite away
  Theirs too shall be as tho' it had not been.

2.

So I said underneath the dusky trees:
  But because I still loved her memory
  I stooped to pluck a pale anemone
And lo! my hand lighted upon heartsease
Not fully blown: while with new life from these
  Fluttered a starry moth that rapidly
  Rose toward the sun: sunlighted flashed on me
Its wings that seemed to throb like heart pulses.
Far far away it flew far out of sight,
  From earth and flowers of earth it passed away
As tho' it flew straight up into the light.
  Then my heart answered me: Thou fool to say
  That she is dead whose night is turned to day,
And whose day shall no more turn back to night.

FROM THE ANTIQUE

It's a weary life, it is, she said –
    Doubly blank in a woman's lot:
I wish and I wish I were a man:
    Or, better then any being, were not:

Were nothing at all in all the world,
    Not a body and not a soul;
Not so much as a grain of dust
    Or a drop of water from pole to pole.

Still the world would wag on the same,
    Still the seasons go and come;
Blossoms bloom as in days of old,
    Cherries ripen and wild bees hum.

None would miss me in all the world,
    How much less would care or weep:
I should be nothing, while all the rest
    Would wake and weary and fall asleep.

SEASONS

In spring time when the leaves are young,
Clear dewdrops gleam like jewels, hung
On boughs the fair birds roost among.

When summer comes with sweet unrest,
Birds weary of their mother's breast,
And look abroad and leave the nest.

In autumn ere the waters freeze,
The swallows fly across the seas: –
If we could fly away with these! –

In winter when the birds are gone,
The sun himself looks starved and wan,
And starved the snow he shines upon.

HOLY INNOCENTS

Sleep, little Baby, sleep,
  The holy Angels love thee,
And guard thy bed, and keep
  A blessed watch above thee.
No spirit can come near
  Nor evil beast to harm thee:
Sleep, Sweet, devoid of fear
  Where nothing need alarm thee.

The Love Which doth not sleep,
  The eternal Arms around thee:
The Shepherd of the sheep
  In perfect love has found thee.
Sleep thro' the holy night,
  Christ-kept from snare and sorrow,
Until thou wake to light
  And love and warmth tomorrow.

A BED OF FORGET-ME-NOTS

Is love so prone to change and rot
We are fain to rear forget-me-not
By measure in a garden plot? –

I love its growth at large and free
By untrod path and unlopped tree,
Or nodding by the unpruned hedge,
Or on the water's dangerous edge
Where flags and meadowsweet blow rank
With rushes on the quaking bank.

Love is not taught in learning's school,
Love is not parcelled out by rule;
Hath curb or call an answer got? –
So free must be forget-me-not.
Give me the flame no dampness dulls,
The passion of the instinctive pulse,
Love steadfast as a fixed star,
Tender as doves with nestlings are,
More large than time, more strong than death:
This all creation travails of –
She groans not for a passing breath –
This is forget-me-not and love.

A CHILLY NIGHT

I rose at the dead of night,
    And went to the lattice alone
To look for my Mother's ghost
    Where the ghostly moonlight shone.

My friends had failed one by one,
    Middle-aged, young, and old,
Till the ghosts were warmed to me
    Than my friends that had grown cold.

I looked and I saw the ghosts
    Dotting plain and mound:
They stood in the blank moonlight,
    But no shadow lay on the ground:
They spoke without a voice
    And they leaped without a sound.

I called: 'O my Mother dear,' –
    I sobbed: 'O my Mother kind,
Make a lonely bed for me
    And shelter it from the wind.

'Tell the others not to come
    To see me night or day:
But I need not tell my friends
    To be sure to keep away.'

My Mother raised her eyes,
    They were blank and could not see:
Yet they held me with their stare
    While they seemed to look at me.

She opened her mouth and spoke;
  I could not hear a word,
While my flesh crept on my bones
  And every hair was stirred.

She knew that I could not hear
  The message that she told
Whether I had long to wait
  Or soon should sleep in the mould:
I saw her toss her shadowless hair
  And wring her hands in the cold.

I strained to catch her words,
  And she strained to make me hear;
But never a sound of words
  Fell on my straining ear.

From midnight to the cockcrow
  I kept my watch in pain
While the subtle ghosts grew subtler
  In the sad night on the wane.

From midnight to the cockcrow
  I watched till all were gone,
Some to sleep in the shifting sea
  And some under turf and stone:
Living had failed and dead had failed,
  And I was indeed alone.

INTROSPECTIVE

I wish it were over the terrible pain,
Pang after pang again and again;
First the shattering ruining blow,
Then the probing steady and slow.

Did I wince? I did not faint:
My soul broke but was not bent;
Up I stand like a blasted tree
By the shore of the shivering sea.

On my boughs neither leaf nor fruit,
No sap in my uttermost root,
Brooding in an anguish dumb
On the short past and the long to come.

Dumb I was when the ruin fell,
Dumb I remain and will never tell:
O my soul I talk with thee
But not another the sight must see.

I did not start when the torture stung,
I did not faint when the torture wrung;
Let it come tenfold if come it must
But I will not groan when I bite the dust.

THE SUMMER IS ENDED

Wreathe no more lilies in my hair,
For I am dying, Sister sweet:
Or if you will for the last time
    Indeed, why make me fair
    Once for my windingsheet.

Pluck no more roses for my breast,
For I like them fade in my prime:
Or if you will, why pluck them still
    That they may share my rest
    Once more, for the last time.

Weep not for me when I am gone,
Dear tender one, but hope and smile:
Or if you cannot choose but weep
    A little while, weep on
    Only a little while.

A STUDY (A SOUL)

She stands as pale as Parian statues stand;
  Like Cleopatra when she turned at bay,
  And felt her strength above the Roman sway,
And felt the aspic writhing in her hand.
Her face is steadfast toward the shadowy land,
  For dim beyond it looms the light of day;
  Her feet are steadfast; all the arduous way
That foot-track hath not wavered on the sand.
She stands there like a beacon thro' the night,
  A pale clear beacon where the storm-drift is;
She stands alone, a wonder deathly white;
She stands there patient, nerved with inner might,
  Indomitable in her feebleness,
Her face and will athirst against the light.

THE HEART KNOWETH ITS OWN BITTERNESS

When all the over-work of life
   Is finished once, and fast asleep
We swerve no more beneath the knife
   But taste that silence cool and deep;
Forgetful of the highways rough,
   Forgetful of the thorny scourge,
   Forgetful of the tossing surge,
Then shall we find it is enough? –

How can we say 'enough' on earth;
   'Enough' with such a craving heart;
I have not found it since my birth,
   But still have bartered part for part.
I have not held and hugged the whole,
   But paid the old to gain the new;
   Much have I paid, yet much is due,
Till I am beggared sense and soul.

I used to labour, used to strive
   For pleasure with a restless will:
Now if I save my soul alive
   All else what matters, good or ill?
I used to dream alone, to plan
   Unspoken hopes and days to come: –
   Of all my past this is the sum:
I will not lean on child of man.

To give, to give, not to receive!
   I long to pour myself, my soul,
Not to keep back or count or leave,
   But king with king to give the whole.
I long for one to stir my deep –

I have had enough of help and gift –
I long for one to search and sift
Myself, to take myself and keep.

You scratch my surface with your pin;
You stroke me smooth with hushing breath; –
Nay pierce, nay probe, nay dig within,
Probe my quick core and sound my depth.
You call me with a puny call,
You talk, you smile, you nothing do;
How should I spend my heart on you,
My heart that so outweighs you all?

Your vessels are by much too strait;
Were I to pour, you could not hold.
Bear with me: I must bear to wait,
A fountain sealed through heat and cold.
Bear with me days or months or years;
Deep must call deep until the end
When friend shall no more envy friend
Nor vex his friend at unawares.

Not in this world of hope deferred,
This world of perishable stuff; –
Eye hath not seen nor ear hath heard
Nor heart conceived that full 'enough':
Here moans the separating sea,
Here harvests fail, here breaks the heart;
There God shall join and no man part,
I full of Christ and Christ of me.

27 August 1857

THREE STAGES

1. *A Pause of Thought*

I looked for that which is not, nor can be,
And hope deferred made my heart sick in truth;
But years must pass before a hope of youth
Is resigned utterly.

I watched and waited with a steadfast will:
And thought the object seemed to flee away
That I so longed for; ever, day by day,
I watched and waited still.

Sometimes I said: This thing shall be no more:
My expectation wearies and shall cease;
I will resign it now and be at peace: –
Yet never gave it o'er.

Sometimes I said: It is an empty name
I long for; to a name why should I give
The peace of all the days I have to live? –
Yet gave it all the same.

Alas, thou foolish one! alike unfit
For health joy and salutary pain;
Thou knowest the chase useless, and again
Turnest to follow it.

2.

My happy dream is finished with,
   My dream in which alone I lived so long.
My heart slept – woe is me, it waketh;
      Was weak – I thought it strong.

Oh weary wakening from a life-true dream:
   Oh pleasant dream from which I wake in pain:
I rested all my trust on things that seem,
      And all my trust is vain.

I must pull down my palace that I built,
   Dig up the pleasure gardens of my soul;
Must change my laughter to sad tears for guilt,
      My freedom to control.

Now all the cherished secrets of my heart,
   Now all my hidden hopes are turned to sin:
Part of my life is dead, part sick, and part
      Is all on fire within.

The fruitless thought of what I might have been
   Haunting me ever will not let me rest:
A cold north wind has withered all my green,
      My sun is in the west.

But where my palace stood, with the same stone,
   I will uprear a shady hermitage;
And there my spirit shall keep house alone,
      Accomplishing its age:

There other garden beds shall lie around
Full of sweet-briar and incense-bearing thyme;
There I will sit, and listen for the sound
Of the last lingering chime.

3.
I thought to deal the death-stroke at a blow,
To give all, once for all, but nevermore; –
Then sit to hear the low waves fret from the shore,
Or watch the silent snow.

'Oh rest,' I thought, 'in silence and the dark;
Oh rest, if nothing else, from head to feet:
Though I may see no more the poppied wheat,
Or sunny soaring lark.

'These chimes are slow, but surely strike at last;
This sand is slow, but surely droppeth thro';
And much there is to suffer, much to do,
before the time is past.

'So will I labour, but will not rejoice:
Will do and bear, but will not hope again;
Gone dead alike to pulses of quick pain,
And pleasure's counterpoise:'

I said so in my heart, and so I thought
My life would lapse, a tedious monotone:
I thought to shut myself, and dwell alone
Unseeking and unsought.

But first I tired, and then my care grew slack;
Till my heart slumbered, may be wandered too: –
I felt the sunshine glow again, and knew
The swallow on its track;

All the birds awoke to building in the leaves,
All buds awake to fullness and sweet scent,
Ah, too, my heart woke unawares, intent
Oh fruitful harvest sheaves.

Full of pulse of life I had deemed was dead,
Full of throb of youth, that I had deemed at rest, –
Alas, I cannot build myself a nest,
I cannot crown my head

With royal purple blossoms for the feast,
Nor flush with laughter, nor exult in song; –
These joys may drift, at time now drift along;
And cease, as once they ceased.

I may pursue, and yet may not attain,
Athirst and painting all the days I live:
Or seem to hold, yet nerve myself to give
What once I gave, again.

THE LAST LOOK

Her face was like an opening rose,
  So bright to look upon;
But now it is like fallen snows
  As cold, as dead, as wan.

Heaven lit with stars is more like her
  Than is this empty crust:
Deaf, dumb, and blind, it cannot stir,
  But crumbles back to dust.

No flower be taken from her bed
  For me, no lock be shorn;
I give her up, the early dead,
  The dead, the newly born:

If I remember her, no need
  Of formal tokens set:
Of hollow token lies indeed
  No need, if I forget.

NEXT OF KIN

The shadows gather round me, while you are in the sun;
My day is almost ended, but yours is just begun:
The winds are singing to us both and the streams are singing still,
And they fill your heart with music, but mine they cannot fill.

Your home is built in sunlight, mine in another day;
Your home is close at hand, sweet friend, but mine is far away:
Your bark is in the haven where you fain would be;
I must launch out into the deep, across the unknown sea.

You, white as dove or lily or spirit of the light;
I, stained and cold and glad to hide in the cold dark night:
You, joy to many a loving heart and light to many eyes;
I, lonely in the knowledge earth is full of vanities.

Yet when your day is over, as mine is nearly done,
And when your race is finished, as mine is almost run,
You, like me, shall cross your hands and bow your graceful head:
Yea, we twain shall sleep together in an equal bed.

ALL SAINTS

They have brought gold and spices to my King,
Incense and precious stuffs and ivory;
O holy Mother mine, what can I bring
That so my Lord may deign to look on me?
They sing a sweeter song than I can sing,
All crowned and glorified exceedingly;
I, bound on earth, weep for my trespassing,–
They sing the song of love in heaven, set free.
Then answered me my Mother, and her voice,
Spake to my heart, yea answered in my heart:
Sing, saith He to the heavens, to earth, Rejoice;
Thou also lift thy heart to Him above;
He seeks not thine, but thee such as thou art,
For lo! His banner over thee is Love.

AUTUMN

Fade, tender lily,
  Fade, O crimson rose,
Fade, every flower,
  Sweetest flower that blows.

Go, chilly Autumn,
  Come, O Winter cold;
Let the green stalks die away
  Into common mould.

Birth follows hard on death,
  Life on withering:
Hasten, we will come the sooner
  Back to pleasant Spring.

IN AN ARTIST'S STUDIO

One face looks out from all his canvasses,
  One selfsame figure sits or walks or leans;
  We found her hidden just behind those screens,
That mirror gave back all her loveliness.
A queen in opal or in ruby dress,
  A nameless girl in freshest summer-greens,
  A saint, an angel – every canvass means
The same one meaning, neither more nor less.
He feeds upon her face by day and night,
  And she with true kind eyes looks back on him
Fair as the moon and joyful as the light:
  Not wan with waiting, not with sorrow dim;
Not as she is, but was when hope shone bright;
  Not as she is, but as she fills his dream.

MAUDE*
A Story for Girls

I.

'A penny for your thoughts,' said Mrs Foster one bright July morning as she entered the sitting-room with a bunch of roses in her hand, and an open letter: 'A penny for your thoughts,' said she, addressing her daughter, who, surrounded by a chaos of stationery, was slipping out of sight some scrawled paper. This observation remaining unanswered, the mother, only too much accustomed to inattention, continued: 'Here is a note from your Aunt Letty; she wants us to go and pass a few days with them. You know Tuesday is Mary's birthday, so they mean to have some young people and cannot dispense with your company.

'Do you think of going?' said Maude at last, having locked her writing-book.

'Yes, dear: even a short stay in the country may do you good, you have looked so pale lately. Don't you feel quite well? Tell me.'

'Oh yes; there is not much the matter, only I am tired and have a headache. Indeed, there is nothing at all the matter; besides, the country may work wonders.'

Half-satisfied, half-uneasy, Mrs Foster asked a few more questions, to have them all answered in the same style; vain questions put to one who, without telling lies, was determined not to tell the truth.

---

* This is the version of Maude used by C.H.Sisson in *Selected Poems* (1985); it is a slightly redacted version of the story, which nonetheless captures the mood and tone of Rossetti's original text.

When once more alone, Maude resumed the occupations which her mother's entrance had interrupted. Her writing-book was neither commonplace-book, album, scrap-book, nor diary; it was a compound of all these, and contained original compositions not intended for the public eye, pet extracts, extraordinary little sketches, and occasional tracts of journal. This choice collection she now proceeded to enrich with the following sonnet:

Yes, I too could face death and never shrink:
But it is harder to bear hated life;
To strive with hands and knees weary of strife;
To drag the heavy chains whose every link
Galls to the bone; to stand upon the brink
Of the deep grave, nor drowse, though it be rife
With sleep; to hold with steady hand the knife
Nor strike home: this is courage as I think.
Surely to suffer is more than to do:
To do is quickly done; to suffer is
Longer and fuller of heart-sicknesses:
Each day's experience testifies of this:
Good deeds are many, but good lives are few;
Thousands taste the full cup; who drains the lees?

having done which she yawned, leaned back in her chair, and wondered how she should fill up the time till dinner.

Maude Foster was just fifteen. Small though not positively short, she might easily be overlooked but would not easily be forgotten. Her figure was slight and well-made, but appeared almost high-shouldered through a habitual shrugging stoop. Her features were regular and pleasing, as a child she had been very pretty; and might have continued so but for a fixed paleness, and an expression, not exactly of pain, but languid and preoccupied to a painful degree. Yet even now, if at any time she became thoroughly aroused and interested, her sleepy eyes would light up with wonderful brilliancy, her cheeks glow with warm colour, her manner become animated, and drawing herself up to her full height she would look more beautiful than ever she did as a child. So Mrs Foster said, and so unhappily Maude knew. She also knew that people thought her clever, and that her little copies of verses were handed about and admired. Touching these same verses, it was the amazement of everyone what could make her poetry so broken-hearted as was mostly the case. Some pronounced that she wrote very foolishly about things she could not possibly understand; some wondered if she really had any secret source of uneasiness; while some simply set her down as affected. Perhaps there was a degree of truth in all these opinions. But I have said enough; the following pages will enable my readers to form their own estimate of Maude's character.

Meanwhile let me transport them to another sitting-room; but this time it will be in the country with a delightful garden look-out.

Mary Clifton was arranging her mother's special nosegay when that lady entered.

'Here, my dear, I will finish doing the flowers. It is time for you to go to meet your aunt and cousin; indeed, if you do not make haste, you will be too late.'

'Thank you, mamma; the flowers are nearly done;' and Mary ran out of the room.

Before long she and her sister were hurrying beneath a burning sun towards the railway station. Through having delayed their start to the very last moment, neither had found time to lay hands on a parasol; but this was little heeded by two healthy girls, full of life and spirits, and longing, moreover, to spy out their friends. Mary wanted one day of fifteen; Agnes was almost a year older: both were well-grown and well-made, with fair hair, blue eyes, and fresh complexions. So far they were alike: what differences existed in other respects remain to be seen. 'How do you do, aunt? How do you do, Maude?' cried Mary, making a sudden dart forward as she discovered our friends, who, having left the station, had already made some progress along the dusty road. Then relinquishing her aunt to Agnes, she seized upon her cousin, and was soon deep in the description of all the pleasures planned for the auspicious morrow.

'We are to do what we like in the morning: I mean, nothing particular is arranged; so I shall initiate you into all the mysteries of the place; all the cats, dogs, rabbits, pigeons, etc.; above all, I must introduce you to a pig, a special *prot*égé of mine: that is, if you are inclined, for you look wretchedly pale; aren't you well, dear?'

'Oh yes, quite well, and you must show me everything. But what are we to do afterwards?'

'Oh! afterwards we are to be intensely grand. All our young friends are coming, and we are to play at round games (you were always clever at round games), and I expect to have great fun. Besides, I have stipulated for unlimited strawberries and cream; also sundry tarts are in course of preparation. By the way, I count on your introducing some new game among us benighted rustics; you who come from dissipated London.'

'I fear I know nothing new, but will do my best. At any rate, I can preside at your toilet, and assist in making you irresistible.'

Mary coloured and laughed; then thought no more of the pretty speech, which sounded as if carefully prepared by her polite cousin. The two made a strong contrast: one was occupied by a thousand shifting thoughts of herself, her friends, her plans, what she must do, and what she would do; the other, whatever might employ her tongue, and to a certain extent her mind, had always an undercurrent of thought intent upon herself.

Arrived at the house, greetings were duly and cordially performed; also an introduction to a new and very fat baby, who received Maude's advances with a howl of intense dismay. The first day of a visit is often no very lively affair: so perhaps all parties heard the clock announce bed-time without much regret.

II.

The young people were assembled in Mary's room, deep in the mysteries of the toilet.

'Here is your wreath, Maude: you must wear it for my sake, and forgive a surreptitious sprig of bay which I have introduced,' said Agnes, adjusting the last white rose, and looking affectionately at her sister and cousin.

Maude was arranging Mary's long fair hair with good-natured anxiety to display it to the utmost advantage.

'One more spray of fuchsia; I was always sure fuchsia would make a beautiful head-dress. There, now you are perfection; only look; look Agnes. Oh, I beg your pardon; thank you; my wreath is very nice, only I have not earned the bay.' She still did not remove it; and when placed on her dark hair it well became the really intellectual character of her face. Her dress was entirely white; simple, fresh, and elegant. Neither she nor Agnes would wear ornaments, but left them to Mary, in whose honour the entertainment was given, and who in all other respects was arrayed like her sister.

In the drawing-room Mary proceeded to set in order the presents received that morning - a handsomely bound Bible from her father, and a small prayer-book with cross and clasp from her mother; a bracelet of Maude's hair from her aunt; a cornelian heart from Agnes; and a pocket *bonbonnière* from her cousin, besides pretty trifles from her little brothers. In the midst of arrangements and re-arrangements the servant entered with a large bunch of lilies from the village school-children and the announcement that Mr and Mrs Savage were just arrived with their six daughters.

Gradually the guests assembled; young and old, pretty and plain; all alike seemingly bent on enjoying themselves; some with gifts, and all with cordial greetings for Mary, for she was a general favourite. There was slim Rosanna Hunt, her scarf arranged with artful negligence to hide a slight protrusion of one shoulder; and sweet Magdalen Ellis, habited as usual in quiet colours. Then came Jane and Alice Deverell, twins so much alike that few besides their parents knew them apart with any certainty; and their fair brother Alexis, who, had he been a girl, would have increased the confusion. There was little Ellen Potter, with a round rosy face like an apple, looking as natural and good-humoured as if, instead of a grand French governess, she had had her own parents with her like most of the other children; and then came three rather haughty-looking Miss Stantons, and pale Hannah Lindley the orphan; and Harriet Eyre, a thought too showy in her dress.

Mary, all life and spirits, hastened to introduce the new-comers to Maude; who, perfectly unembarrassed, bowed and uttered little speeches with the manner of a practical woman of the world; while the genuine, unobtrusive courtesy of Agnes did more towards making their guests comfortable than the eager good nature of her sister, or the correct breeding of her cousin.

At length the preliminaries were all accomplished, everyone having found a seat, or being otherwise satisfactorily disposed of. The elders of the party were grouped here and there, talking and looking on; the very small children were accommodated in the adjoining apartment with a gigantic Noah's Ark: and the rest of the young people being at liberty to amuse themselves as fancy might prompt, a general appeal was made to Miss Foster for some game, novel, entertaining, and ingenious; or, some of the more diffident hinted, easy.

'I really know nothing new,' said Maude; 'you must have played at "Proverbs", "What's my thought like", "How do you like it", and "Magic music" :- or stay, there is one thing we can try - "*Bouts-rimés*".'

'What?' asked Mary.

'"*Bouts-rimés*": it is very easy. Some one gives rhymes – mamma can do that – and then all of us fill them up as we think fit. A sonnet is the best form to select; but, if you wish, we could try eight, or even four lines.'

'But I am certain I could not make a couplet,' said Mary, laughing. 'Of course you would get on capitally, and Agnes might manage very well, and Magdalen can do anything; but it is quite beyond me: do pray think of something more suitable to my capacity.'

'Indeed I have nothing else to propose. This is very much better than mere common games; but if you will not try it, that ends the matter'; and Maude leaned back in her chair.

'I hope-' began Mary; but Agnes interposed:

'Suppose some of us attempt "*Bouts-rimés*"; and you meanwhile can settle what we shall do afterwards. Who is ready to test her poetic powers? – What, no one? Oh, Magdalen, pray join Maude and me.'

This proposal met with universal approbation, and the three girls retreated to a side-table, Mary, who supplied the rhymes, exacting a promise that only one sonnet should be composed. Before the next game was fixed upon, the three following productions were submitted for judgment to the discerning public. The first was by Agnes:

> Would that I were a turnip white,
> Or raven black,
> Or miserable hack
> Dragging a cab from left to right;
> Or would I were the showman of a sight,

Or weary donkey with a laden back,
Or racer in a sack,
Or freezing traveller on an Alpine height;
Or would I were straw-catching as I drown,
(A wretched landsman I who cannot swim),
Or watching a lone vessel sink,
Rather than writing; I would change my pink
Gauze for a hideous yellow satin gown,
With deep-cut scalloped edges and a rim.

'Indeed, I had no idea of the sacrifice you were making,' observed Maude. 'You did it with such heroic equanimity. Might I, however, venture to hint that my sympathy with your sorrows would have been greater had they been expressed in metre.' 'There's gratitude for you,' cried Agnes gaily; 'what have you to expect, Magdalen?' and she went on to read her friend's sonnet.

I fancy the good fairies dressed in white,
Glancing like moon-beams through the shadows black;
Without much work to do for king or hack.
Training perhaps some twisted branch aright;
Or sweeping faded Autumn leaves from sight
To foster embryo life; or binding back
Stray tendrils; or in ample bean-pod sack
Bringing wild honey from the rocky height;
Or fishing for a fly lest it should drown;
Or teaching water-lily heads to swim,
Fearful that sudden rain might make them sink;
Or dyeing the pale rose a warmer pink;
Or wrapping lilies in their leafy gown,
Yet letting the white peep beyond the rim.

'Well, Maude?'

'Well, Agnes; Miss Ellis is too kind to feel gratified at hearing that her verses make me tremble for my own: but such as they are, listen:

> Some ladies dress in muslin full and white,
> Some gentlemen in cloth succinct and black;
> Some patronise a dog-cart, some a hack,
> Some think a painted clarence only right.
> Youth is not always such a pleasing sight:
> Witness a man with tassels on his back;
> Or woman in a great-coat like a sack
> Towering above her sex with horrid height.
> If all the world were water fit to drown
> There are some whom you would not teach to swim;
> Rather enjoying if you saw them sink;
> Certain old ladies dressed in girlish pink,
> With roses and geraniums on their gown:
> Go to the Bason, poke them o'er the rim.'

'What a very odd sonnet,' said Mary after a slight pause; 'but surely men don't wear tassels.'

Her cousin smiled. 'You must allow for poetical licence; and I have literally seen a man in Regent Street wearing a sort of hooded cloak with one tassel. Of course everyone will understand the Bason to mean the one in St James' Park.'

'With these explanations your sonnet is comprehensible,' said Mary; and Magdalen added with unaffected pleasure: 'And without them it was by far the best of the three.'

Maude now exerted herself to amuse the party; and soon proved that ability was not lacking. Game after game was proposed and played at; and her fun seemed inexhaustible, for nothing was thought too nonsensical or too noisy for the occasion. Her good humour and animation were infectious: Miss Stanton incurred forfeits with the blandest smile; Hannah Lindley blushed and dimpled as she had not done for many months, Rosanna never perceived the derangement of her scarf; little Ellen exulted in freedom from school-room trammels; the twins guessed each other's thoughts with marvellous facility; Magdalen laughed aloud; and even Harriet Eyre's dress looked scarcely too gay for such an entertainment. Well was it for Mrs Clifton that the strawberries, cream, and tarts had been supplied with no niggard hand: and very meagre was the remnant left when the party broke up at a late hour.

III.

Agnes and Mary were discussing the pleasures of the preceding evening as they sat over the unusually late breakfast, when Maude joined them. Salutations being exchanged and refreshments supplied to the last comer, the conversation was renewed.

'Who did you think was the prettiest girl in the room last night? our charming selves, of course, excepted,' asked Mary; 'Agnes and I cannot agree on this point.'

'Yes,' said her sister; 'we quite agree as to mere prettiness; only I maintain that Magdalen is infinitely more attractive than half the handsome people one sees. There is so much sense in her face and such sweetness. Besides, her eyes are really beautiful.' 'Miss Ellis has a characteristic countenance; but she appeared to me very far from the belle of the evening. Rosanna Hunt has much more regular features.'

'Surely you don't think Rosanna prettier than Jane and Alice,' interrupted Mary; 'I suppose I never look at those two without fresh pleasure.'

'They have good fair complexions, eyes, and hair, certainly,' and Maude glanced rather pointedly at her unconscious cousin; 'but to me they have a wax-dollish air which is quite unpleasant. I think one of the handsomest faces in the room was Miss Stanton's.'

'But she has such a disagreeable expression,' rejoined Mary hastily: then colouring, she half-turned towards her sister, who looked grave, but did not speak.

A pause ensued; and then Agnes said, 'I remember how prejudiced I felt against Miss Stanton when first she came to live here, for her appearance and manners are certainly unattractive: and how ashamed of myself I was when we heard that last year, through all the bitterly cold weather, she rose at six, though she never has a fire in her room, that she might have time before breakfast to make clothes for some of the poorest people in the village. And in the spring, when the scarlet fever was about, her mother would not let her go near the sick children for fear of contagion; so she saved up all her pocket money to buy wine and soup and such things for them as they recovered .'

'I dare say she is very good,' said Maude; 'but that does not make her pleasing. Besides, the whole family have that disagreeable expression, and I suppose they are not all paragons. But you have both finished breakfast, and make me ashamed by your diligence. What is that beautiful piece of work?'

The sisters looked delighted: 'I am so glad you like it, dear Maude. Mary and I are embroidering a cover for the lectern in our church; but we feared you might think the ground dull.'

'Not at all; I prefer those quiet shades. Why, how well you do it: is it not very difficult? Let me see if I understand the devices. There is the Cross and the Crown of Thorns; and those must be the keys of St Peter, with, of course, the sword of St Paul. Do the flowers mean anything?'

'I am the Rose of Sharon and the Lily of the Valley,' answered Agnes, pointing. 'That is the Balm of Gilead – at least, it is what we will call so; there are myrrh and hyssop, and that is a palm-branch. The border is to be vine-leaves and grapes; with fig leaves at the corners, thanks to Mary's suggestions. Would you like to help us? There is plenty of room at the frame.'

'No; I should not do it well enough, and have no time to learn, as we go home to-morrow. How I envy you,' she continued in a low voice, as if speaking rather to herself than to her hearers: 'you who live in the country, and are exactly what you appear, and never wish for what you do not possess. I am sick of display, and poetry, and acting.'

'You do not act,' replied Agnes, warmly. 'I never knew a more sincere person. One difference between us is that you are less healthy and far more clever than I am. And this reminds me: Miss Savage begged me to ask you for some verses to put in her album. Would you be so very obliging? Any that you have by you would do.'

'She can have the sonnet I wrote last night.'

Agnes hesitated: 'I could not well offer her that, because-'

'Why? she does not "tower". Oh! I suppose she has some reprehensible old lady in her family, and so might feel hurt at my lynch-law.'

PART SECOND

I.

Rather more than a year had elapsed since Maude parted from her cousins; and now she was expecting their arrival in London every minute: for Mrs Clifton, unable to leave her young family, had gratefully availed herself of Mrs Foster's offer to receive Agnes and Mary during the early winter months, that they might take music and dancing lessons with their cousin .

At length the rumbling of an approaching cab was heard; then a loud knock and ring. Maude started up: but instead of running out to meet her guests, began poking vigorously at the fire, which soon sent a warm, cheerful light through the apartment, enabling her, when they entered, to discern that Agnes had a more womanly air than at their last meeting, that

Mary had outgrown her sister, and that both were remarkably good-looking.

'First let me show you your room; and then we can settle comfortably to tea; we are not to wait for mamma. She thought you would not mind sleeping together, as our house is so small; and I have done my best to arrange things for your taste, for I know of old how you have only one taste between you. Look, my room is next yours, so we can help each other very cosily: only pray don't think of unpacking now; there will be plenty of time this evening, and you must be famished: come.'

But Agnes lingered still, eager to thank her cousin for the good-natured forethought which had robbed her own apartment of flower-vases and inkstand for the accommodation of her guests. The calls of Mary's appetite were however imperious; and very soon the sisters were snugly settled on a sofa by the fire, while Maude, in a neighbouring arm-chair, made tea.

'How long it seems since my birthday party,' said Mary, as soon as the eatables had in some measure restored her social powers. 'Why, Maude, you are grown quite a woman; but you look more delicate than ever, and very thin: do you still write verses? 'Then without waiting for a reply: 'Those which you gave Miss Savage for her album were very much admired; and Magdalen Ellis wished at the time for an autograph copy, only she had not courage to trouble you. But perhaps you are not aware that poor Magdalen has done with albums and such like, at least for the present: she has entered on her noviciate in the Sisterhood of Mercy established near our house.'

'Why poor?' said Maude. 'I think she is very happy.'

'Surely you would not like such a life,' rejoined her cousin. 'They have not proper clothes on their beds, and never go out without a thick veil, which must half-blind them. All day long they are at prayers, or teaching children, or attending the sick, or making things for the poor, or something. Is that to your taste?'

Maude half-sighed; and then answered: 'You cannot imagine me either fit or inclined for such a life; still I can perceive that those who are so are very happy. When I was preparing for confirmation, Mr Paulson offered me a district, but I did not like the trouble, and mamma thought me too unwell to be regular. I have regretted it since, though yet I don't fancy I ever could have talked to the poor people or have done the slightest good. Yes, I continue to write now and then as the humour seizes me; and if Miss Ellis-'

'Sister Magdalen,' whispered Agnes.

'If Sister Magdalen will accept it, I will try and find her something admissible even within convent walls. But let us change the subject. On Thursday we are engaged to tea at Mrs Strawdy's. There will be no sort of party, so we need not dress or take any trouble.'

'Will my Aunt go with us?' asked Agnes.

'No. Poor mamma has been ailing for some time, and is by no means strong; so, as Mrs Strawdy is an old schoolfellow of hers, and a most estimable person, she thinks herself justified in consigning you to my guardianship. On Saturday we must go shopping, as Aunt Letty says you are to get your winter things in London; and I can get mine at the same time. On Sunday- or does either of you dislike Cathedral services?'

Agnes declared they were her delight; and Mary, who had never attended any, expressed great pleasure at the prospect of hearing what her sister preferred to all secular music.

'Very well,' continued Maude; 'we will go to St Andrew's then, and you shall be introduced to a perfect service; or, at any rate, to perhaps the nearest English approach to vocal perfection. But you know you are to be quite at home here; so we have not arranged any particular plans of amusement, but mean to treat you like ourselves. And now it is high time for you to retire.'

II.

When Thursday arrived Agnes and Mary were indisposed with colds; so Mrs Foster insisted that her daughter should make their excuses to Mrs Strawdy. In a dismal frame of mind, Maude, assisted by her sympathising cousins, performed her slight preliminary toilet.

'You have no notion of the utter dreariness of this kind of invitation. I counted on your helping me through the evening, and now you fail me. Thank you, Mary; I shall not waste *eau de Cologne* on my handkerchief. Good-night both: mind you go to bed early, and get up quite well to-morrow. Good-night.'

The weather was foggy and raw as Maude stepped into the street; and proved anything but soothing to a temper already fretted; so by the time she had arrived at her destination, re moved her walking things, saluted her hostess, and apologised for her cousins, her countenance had assumed an expression neither pleased nor pleasing.

'Let me present my nieces to you, my dear, said Mrs Strawdy, taking her young friend by the hand and leading her towards the fire: 'This is Miss Mowbray, or, as you must call her, Annie; that is Caroline, and that Sophy. They have heard so much of you, that any further introduction is needless'; here Maude bowed rather stiffly: 'but as you are early people, you will excuse our commencing with tea, after which we shall have leisure for amusement.'

There was nothing so genuinely kind and simple as Mrs Strawdy's manner, that even Maude felt mollified, and resolved on doing her best not only towards suppressing all appearance of yawns, but also towards bearing her part in the conversation. 'My cousins will regret their indisposition more than ever, when they learn of how much pleasure it has deprived them,' said she, civilly addressing Miss Mowbray.

A polite bend, smile, and murmur formed the sole response, and once more a subject had to be started.

'Have you been very gay lately? I begin to acquire the reputation of an invalid; and so my privacy is respected.'

Annie coloured and looked excessively embarrassed; at last she answered in a low hesitating voice: 'We go out extremely little, partly because we never dance.'

'Nor I either; it really is too fatiguing: yet a ball-room is no bad place for a mere spectator. Perhaps, though, you prefer the Theatre?'

'We never go to the play,' rejoined Miss Mowbray, looking more and more uncomfortable.

Maude ran on: 'Oh, I beg your pardon, you do not approve of such entertainments. I never go, but only for want of some one to take me.' Then addressing Mrs Strawdy: 'I think you know my aunt, Mrs Clifton?'

'I visited her years ago with your mamma,' was the answer: 'when you were quite a little child. I hope she continues in good health. Pray remember me to her and to Mr Clifton when you write.'

'With pleasure. She has a large family now, eight children.'

'That is indeed a large family,' rejoined Mrs Strawdy, intent meanwhile on dissecting a cake with mathematical precision: 'you must try a piece, it is Sophy's own manufacture.'

Despairing of success in this quarter, Maude now directed her attention to Caroline, whose voice she not heard once in the course of the evening.

'I hope you will favour us with some music after tea; in fact, I can take no denial. You look too blooming to plead a cold, and I feel certain you will not refuse to indulge my love for sweet sounds: of your ability to do so I have heard elsewhere.'

'I shall be most happy; only you must favour us in return.'

'I will do my best,' answered Maude, somewhat encouraged; 'but my own performances are very poor. Are you fond of German songs? they form my chief resource.'

'Yes, I like them much.'

Baffled in this quarter also, Miss Foster wanted courage to attack Sophy, whose countenance promised more cake than conversation. The meal seemed endless: she fidgeted under the table with her fingers; pushed about a stool on the noiselessly soft carpet until it came in contact with someone's foot; and at last fairly deprived Caroline of her third cup of coffee, by opening the piano and claiming the fulfilment of her promise.

The young lady complied with obliging readiness. She sang some simple airs, mostly religious, not indeed with much expression, but in a voice clear and warbling as a bird's. Maude felt consoled for all the contrarieties of the day; and was bargaining for one more song before taking Caroline's place at the instrument, when the door opened to admit Mrs and Miss Savage; who having only just reached town, and hearing from Mrs Foster that her daughter was at the house of a mutual friend, resolved on begging the hospitality of Mrs Strawdy, and renewing their acquaintance.

Poor Maude's misfortunes now came thick and fast. Seated between Miss Savage and Sophia Mowbray, she was attacked on either hand with questions concerning her verses. In the first place, did she continue to write? Yes. A flood of ecstatic compliments followed this admission: she was so young, so much admired, and, poor thing, looked so delicate. It was quite affecting to think of her lying awake at night meditating those sweet verses- ('I sleep like a top,' Maude put in, drily)- which so delighted her friends, and would so charm the public if only Miss Foster could be induced to publish. At last the bystanders were called upon to intercede for a recitation.

Maude coloured with displeasure; a hasty answer was rising to her lips, when the absurdity of her position flashed across her mind so forcibly that, almost unable to check a laugh in the midst of her annoyance, she put her handkerchief to her mouth. Miss Savage, impressed with a notion that her request was about to be complied with, raised her hand, imploring silence; and settled herself in a listening attitude.

'You will excuse me,' Maude at last said very coldly; 'I could not think of monopolising every one's attention. Indeed you are extremely good, but you must excuse me.' And here Mrs Savage interposed, desiring her daughter not to tease Miss Foster; and Mrs Strawdy seconded her friend's arguments by a hint that supper would make its appearance in a few minutes.

Finally the maid announced that Miss Foster was 'fetched', and Maude, shortening her adieus and turning a deaf ear to Annie's suggestions that their acquaintance should not terminate with the first meeting, returned home dissatisfied with her circumstances, her friends, and herself.

III.

It was Christmas Eve. All day long Maude and her cousins were hard at work putting up holly and mistletoe in wreaths, festoons, or bunches, wherever the arrangement of the rooms admitted of such embellishment. The picture-frames were hidden behind foliage and bright berries; the bird-cages were stuck as full of green as though it had been Summer. A fine sprig of holly was set apart as a centre-bit for the pudding of next day: scratched hands and injured gowns were disregarded: hour after hour the noisy bustle raged: until Mrs Foster, hunted from place to place by her young relatives, heard, with inward satisfaction, that the decorations were completed.

After tea Mary set the backgammon board in array and challenged her aunt to their customary evening game: Maude, complaining of a headache, and promising either to wrap herself in a warm shawl or to go to bed, went to her room, and Agnes, listening to the rattle of the dice, at last came to the conclusion that her presence was not needed downstairs, and resolved to visit the upper regions. Thinking that her cousin was lying down tired and might have fallen asleep, she forbore knocking; but opened the door softly and peeped in.

Maude was seated at a table surrounded by the old chaos of stationery; before her lay the locking manuscript-book, into which she had just copied something. That day she had appeared more than usually animated: and now supporting her forehead upon her hand, her eyes cast down till the long lashes nearly rested upon her cheeks, she looked pale, languid, almost in pain. She did not move, but let her visitor come close to her without speaking. Agnes thought she was crying.

'Dear Maude, you have overtired yourself. Indeed, for all our sakes, you should be more careful': here Agnes passed her arm affectionately round her friend's neck: 'I hoped to find you fast asleep, and instead of this you have been writing in the cold.'

'You will stay to Communion to-morrow?' asked Maude after a short silence, and without replying to her cousin's remarks; even these few words seemed to cost her an effort.

'Of course I shall; why, it is Christmas Day: at least I trust to do so. Mary and I have been thinking how nice it will be for us all to receive together: so I want you to promise that you will pray for us at the Altar, as I shall for you. Will you?'

'I shall not receive to-morrow,' answered Maude; then hurrying on as if to prevent the other from remonstrating: 'No: at least I will not profane Holy Things; I will not add this to all the rest. I have gone over and over again, thinking I should come right in time, and I do not come right. I will go no more.'

Agnes turned quite pale: 'Stop,' she said, interrupting her cousin: 'stop; you cannot mean- you do not know what you are saying. You will go no more? Only think if the struggle is so hard now, what it will be when you reject all help.'

'I do not struggle.'

'You are ill to-night,' rejoined Agnes very gently; 'you are tired and over-excited. Take my advice, dear; say your prayers and get to bed. But do not be very long; if there is anything you miss and will tell me of, I will say it in your stead. Don't think me unfeeling: I was once on the very point of acting as you propose. I was perfectly wretched: harassed and discouraged on all sides. But then it struck me- you won't be angry?- that it was so ungrateful to follow my own fancies, instead of at least endeavouring to do God's Will: and so foolish too; for if our safety is not in obedience, where is it?'

Maude shook her head: 'Your case is different. Whatever your faults may be (not that I perceive any), you are trying to correct them; your own conscience tells you that. But I am not trying. No one will say that I cannot avoid putting myself forward and displaying my verses. Agnes, you must admit so much.'

Deep-rooted indeed was that vanity which made Maude take pleasure, on such an occasion, in proving the force of arguments directed against herself. Still Agnes would not yield; but resolutely did battle for the truth.

'If hitherto it has been so, let it be so no more. It is not too late; besides, think for one moment what will be the end of this. We must all die: what if you keep to your resolution, and do as you have said, and receive the Blessed Sacrament no more?'-Her eyes filled with tears.

Maude's answer came in a subdued tone: 'I do not mean never to communicate again. You remember Mr Paulson told us last Sunday that sickness and suffering are sent for our correction. I suffer very much. Perhaps a time will come when these will have done their work on me also; when I shall be purified indeed and weaned from the world. Who knows? the lost have been found, the dead quickened.' She paused as if in thought; then continued: 'You partake of the Blessed Sacrament in peace, Agnes, for you are good; and Mary, for she is harmless: but your conduct cannot serve to direct mine, because I am neither the one nor the other. Some day I may be fit again to approach the Holy Altar, but till then I will at least refrain from dishonouring it.'

Agnes felt almost indignant. 'Maude, how can you talk so? this is not reverence. You cannot mean that for the present you will indulge vanity and display; that you will court admiration and applause; that you will take your fill of pleasure until sickness, or it may be death, strips you of temptation and sin together. Forgive me; I am sure you never meant this: yet what else does a deliberate resolution to put off doing right come to?- and if you are determined at once to do your best, why deprive yourself of the appointed means of grace? Dear Maude, think better of it'; and Agnes knelt beside her cousin, and laid her head against her bosom.

But still Maude, with a sort of desperate wilfulness, kept saying: 'It is of no use; I cannot go to-morrow; it is of no use.' She hid her face, leaning upon the table and weeping bitterly; while Agnes, almost discouraged, quitted the room.

Maude, once more alone, sat for some time just as her cousin left her. Gradually the thick, low sobs became more rare; she was beginning to feel sleepy. At last she roused herself with an effort, and commenced undressing; then it struck her that her prayers had still to be said. The idea of beginning them frightened her, yet she could not settle to sleep without saying something. Strange prayers they must have been, offered with a divided heart and a reproachful conscience. Still they were said at length; and Maude lay down harassed, wretched, remorseful, everything but penitent. She was nearly asleep, nearly unconscious of her troubles, when the first stroke of midnight sounded.

PART THIRD

I

Agnes Clifton to Maude Foster

12th June 18–

My dear Maude,

Mamma has written to my aunt that Mary's marriage is fixed for the 4th of next month: but as I fear we cannot expect you both so many days before the time, I also write, hoping that you at least will come without delay. At any rate, I shall be at the station to-morrow afternoon with a chaise for your luggage, so pray take pity on my desolate condition, and avail yourself of the three o'clock train. As we are both bridesmaids elect, I thought it would be very nice for us to be dressed alike, so have procured double quantity of everything; thus you will perceive no pretence remains for your lingering in smoky London.

You will be amused when you see Mary. I have already lost my companion. Mr Herbert calls at least once a day, but sometimes oftener; so all day long Mary is on the alert. She takes much more interest in the roses over the porch than was formerly the case; the creepers outside the windows require continual training, not to say hourly care: I tell her the constitution of the garden must have become seriously weakened lately. One morning I caught her before the glass, trying the effect of syringa (the English orange-blossom, you know) in her hair. She looked such a darling. I hinted how flattered Mr Herbert would feel when I told him; which provoked her to offer a few remarks on old maids. Was it not a shame?

Last Thursday Magdalen Ellis was finally received into the Sisterhood of Mercy. I wished much to be present, but could not, as the whole affair was conducted quite privately; only her parents were admitted. However, I made interest for a lock of her beautiful hair, which I prize highly. It makes me sad to look at it; yet I know she has chosen well; and will, if she perseveres, receive hereafter an abundant recompense for all she has forgone here. Sometimes I think whether such a life can be suited to me; but then I could not leave mamma: indeed, that is just what Magdalen felt so much. I met her yesterday walking with some poor children. Her veil was down, nearly hiding her face; still I fancy she looked thoughtful, but very calm and happy. She says she always prays for me, and asked my prayers; so I begged her to remember you and Mary. Then she inquired how you are; desiring her kindest love to you, and assuring me she makes no doubt your name will be known at some future period: but checking herself almost immediately, she added that she could fancy you very different, as pale Sister Maude. This surprised me, I can fancy nothing of the sort. Then, having nearly reached my home, we parted.

What a document I have composed; I who have not one minute to spare from Mary's trousseau. Will you give my love to my aunt; and request her from me to permit your immediately coming to your affectionate cousin,

Agnes M. Clifton.

P.S.– Mary would doubtless send a message were she in the room; I conjecture her to be lurking about somewhere on the watch. Good-bye: or rather, Come.

– Maude handed the letter to her mother. 'Can you spare me, mamma? I should like to go, but not if it is to inconvenience you.'

'Certainly you shall go, my dear. It is a real pleasure to hear you express interest on some point, and you cannot be with anyone I approve of more than Agnes. But you must make haste with the packing now. I will come and help you in a few minutes.'

Still Maude lingered. 'Did you see about Magdalen? I wonder what made her think of me as a Sister. It is very nice of her; but then she is so good she never can conceive what I am like. Mamma, should you mind my being a nun?'

'Yes, my dear; it would make me miserable. But for the present take my advice and hurry a little, or the train will leave without you.'

Thus urged, Maude proceeded to bundle various miscellaneous goods into a trunk; the only article on the safety of which she bestowed much thought being the present destined for Mary: a sofa-pillow worked in glowing shades of wool and silk. This she wrapped carefully in cloth, and laid at the bottom: then over it all else was heaped without much ceremony. Many were the delays occasioned by things mislaid, which must be looked for, ill-secured, which must be re-arranged; or remembered too late, which yet could not be dispensed with, and so must be crammed in somewhere. At length, however, the tardy preparations were completed; and Maude, enveloped in two shawls, though it was the height of summer, stepped into a cab; promising strict conformity to her mother's injunction that both the windows should be kept closed.

Half-an-hour had not elapsed when another cab drove up to the door; and out of it Maude was lifted perfectly insensible. She had been overturned; and, though no limb was broken, had neither stirred nor spoken since the accident.

II

Maude Foster to Agnes Clifton

2nd July 18–

My dear Agnes,
You have heard of my mishap? it keeps me not bed-ridden, but sofa-ridden. My side is dreadfully hurt; I looked at it this morning for the first time, but hope never again to see so shocking a sight. The pain now and then is extreme; though not always so; sometimes, in fact, I am unconscious of any injury.

Will you convey my best love and wishes to Mary, and tell her how much I regret being away from her at such a time, especially as mamma will not hear of leaving me.

The surgeon comes twice a day to dress my wounds; still, all the burden of nursing falls on poor mamma. How I wish you were here to help us both; we should find plenty to say.

But, perhaps, ere many months are past I shall be up and about, when we may go together on a visit to Mary; a most delightful possibility. By the way, how I should love a baby of hers, and what a pretty little creature it ought to be. Do you think Mr Herbert handsome? hitherto I have only had a partial opinion.

Ugh, my side! it gives an awful twinge now and then. You need not read my letter; but I must write it, for I am unable to do anything else. Did the pillow reach safely? It gave me so much pleasure to work it for Mary, who, I hope, likes it. At all events, if not to her taste, she may console herself with the reflection that it is unique; for the pattern was my own designing.

Here comes dinner; good-bye. When will anything so welcome as your kind face gladden the eyes of your affectionate Maude Foster?

P.S. – I have turned tippler lately on port wine three times a day. 'To keep you up,' says my doctor: while I obstinately refuse to be kept up, but insist on becoming weaker and weaker. Mind you write me a full history of your grand doings on a certain occasion: not omitting a detailed account of the lovely bride, her appearance, deportment, and toilet. Good-bye once more: when shall I see you all again?

III

Three weeks had passed away. A burning sun seemed baking the very dust in the streets, and sucking the last remnant of moisture from the straw spread in front of Mrs Foster's house, when the sound of a low muffled ring was heard in the sick-room and Maude, now entirely confined to her bed, raising herself on one arm, looked eagerly towards the door; which opened to admit a servant with the welcome announcement that Agnes had arrived.

After tea Mrs Foster, almost worn out with fatigue, went to bed, leaving her daughter under the care of their guest. The first greetings between the cousins had passed sadly enough. Agnes perceived at a glance that Maude was, as her last letter hinted, in a most alarming state; while the sick girl, well aware of her condition, received her friend with an emotion which showed she felt it might be for the last time. But soon her spirits rallied. 'I shall enjoy our evening together so much, Agnes,' said she, speaking now quite cheerfully. 'You must tell me all the news. Have you heard from Mary since your last despatch to me?'

'Mamma received a letter this morning before I set off; and she sent it, hoping to amuse you. Shall I read it aloud?'

'No; let me have it myself.' Her eye travelled rapidly down the well-filled pages, comprehending at a glance all the tale of happiness. Mr and Mrs Herbert were at Scarborough; they would thence proceed to the Lakes; and thence, most probably, homewards, though a prolonged tour was mentioned as just possible. But both plans seemed alike pleasing to Mary; for she was full of her husband, and both were equally connected with him.

Maude smiled as paragraph after paragraph enlarged on the same topic. At last she said: 'Agnes, if you could not be yourself, but must become one of us three: I don't mean as to goodness, of course, but merely as regards circumstances, would you change with Sister Magdalen, with Mary, or with me?'

'Not with Mary, certainly. Neither should I have courage to change with you; I never should bear pain so well: nor yet with Sister Magdalen; for I want her fervour of devotion. So at present I fear you must even put up with me as I am. Will that do?'

There was a pause. A fresh wind had sprung up, and the sun was setting.

At length Maude resumed: 'Do you recollect last Christmas Eve when I was so wretched, what shocking things I said? How I rejoice that my next Communion was not indeed delayed till sickness had stripped me of temptation and sin together.'

'Did I say that? It was very harsh.'

'Not harsh: it was just and right as far as it went; only something more was required. But I never told you what altered me. The truth is, for a time I avoided as much as possible frequenting our parish church, for fear of remarks. Mamma, knowing how I love St Andrew's, let me go there very often by myself, because the walk is too long for her. I wanted resolution to do right; yet, believe me, I was very miserable; how I could say my prayers at that period is a mystery. So matters went on; till one day as I was returning from a shop, I met Mr Paulson. He enquired immediately whether I had been staying in the country. Of course I answered, No. Had I been ill? again, No. Then gradually the whole story came out. I never shall forget the shame of my admissions; each word seemed forced from me, yet at last, all was told. I will not repeat all we said then, and on a subsequent occasion when he saw me at church: the end was, that I partook of the Holy Communion on Easter Day. That was indeed a Feast.'

Then changing the conversation abruptly, Maude said: 'Agnes, it would only pain mamma to look over everything if I die; will you examine my verses and destroy what I evidently never intended to be seen. They might all be thrown away together, only mamma is so fond of them. What will she do?' – and the poor girl hid her face in the pillows.

'But is there no hope, then?'

'Not the slightest, if you mean of recovery; and she does not know it. Don't go away when all's over, but do what you can to comfort her. I have been her misery from my birth till now; there is no time to do better, but you must leave me, please; for I feel completely exhausted. Or, stay one moment. I saw Mr Paulson again this morning, and he promised to come to-morrow to administer the Blessed Sacrament to me; so I count on you and mamma receiving with me, for the last time perhaps: will you?'

'Yes, dear Maude. But you are so young, don't give up hope. And now would you like me to remain here during the night? I can establish myself quite comfortably on your sofa.'

'Thank you, but it could only make me restless. Good-night, my own dear Agnes.'

'Good-night, dear Maude. I trust to rise early to-morrow, that I may be with you all the sooner.' So they parted.

That morrow never dawned for Maude Foster.

Agnes proceeded to perform the task imposed upon her, with scrupulous anxiety to carry out her friend's wishes. The locked book she never opened; but had it placed in Maude's coffin, with all its words of folly, sin, vanity; and, she humbly trusted, of true penitence also. She next collected the scraps of paper found in her cousin's desk and portfolio, or lying loose upon the table; and proceeded to examine them. Many of these were mere fragments, many half-effaced pencil scrawls, some written on torn backs of letters, and some full of incomprehensible abbreviations.

Agnes was astonished at the variety of Maude's compositions. Piece after piece she committed to the flames, fearful lest any should be preserved not intended for general perusal: but it cost her a pang to do so; and to see how small a number remained for Mrs Foster. Of two only she took copies for herself.

The first was evidently composed subsequently to Maude's accident:

Fade, tender lily,
    Fade, O crimson rose,
Fade every flower,
    Sweetest flower that blows.

Go, chilly Autumn,
    Come, O Winter cold;
Let the green stalks die away
    Into common mould.

Birth follows hard on death,
    Life on withering.
Hasten, we shall come the sooner
    Back to pleasant Spring.

The other was a sonnet, dated the morning before her death:

What is it Jesus saith unto the soul?
'Take up the Cross, and come, and follow Me.'
This word He saith to all; no man may be
    Without the Cross, wishing to win the goal.
    Then take it bravely up, setting thy whole
Body to bear; it will not weigh on thee
Beyond thy utmost strength: take it; for He
    Knoweth when thou art weak, and will control
The powers of darkness that thou need'st not fear.
    He will be with thee, helping, strengthening,
Until it is enough: for lo, the day
Cometh when He shall call thee: thou shalt hear
    His Voice that says: 'Winter is past, and Spring
Is come; arise, My Love, and come away.'

Agnes cut one long tress from Maude's head; and on her return home laid it in the same paper with the lock of

Magdalen's hair. These she treasured greatly, and, gazing on them, would long and pray for the hastening of that eternal morning which shall reunite in God those who in Him, or for His sake, have parted here.

Amen for us all.

THE END

INDEX OF TITLES